© Myron T. Powell, 2021

ALL RIGHTS RESERVED
No part of this publication may be reproduced, stored in a retrieval system, or transmitted, in any form or by any means–electronic, mechanical, photocopying, recording, or otherwise–without prior written permission from the author.

ISBN: 9798542496993

Volume 3, *God is in Trouble,* **Psalms 40-62**

Myron T. Powell
3715 N. 104th Ave.
Omaha, NE 68134
(402) 614-4811
myron.powell@thechurchofomaha.com

Without God, I would be hopeless. I thank Him for the anointing and ability to write this book.

Thank you for purchasing this third volume. I trust you will enjoy your journey through Psalms 40-62 and hope you enjoy reading about them as much as I enjoyed writing about them.

Thank you, Erica Raymond, Keith Mierzwiak, Samuel Cuellar III, Terry and Laurel James, and Sal Melendrez, for your help transcribing my preaching notes, editing, and providing your feedback and collaboration to make this book readable and understandable.

Thank you, Pastor Phillip Harrelson, for writing the foreword. Your mentorship and friendship are both invaluable to me. You are a true expositor of the Holy Scripture par excellence.

Thank you, Pastor Paul Kinney, for writing the epilogue. Your investment is timeless and eternal, and I am eternally grateful for your influence.

I dedicate this third volume to you, the reader. May the Lord open your understanding that you may comprehend His Holy Word accurately.

Prologue

"God is in trouble" almost sounds sacrilegious until you consider the number of psalms that say so. One of the main ones is included in this third volume, Psalm 46:1, "**<u>God is</u>** *our refuge and strength, a very present help **<u>in trouble</u>***" (emphasis mine).

The idea for using *God is in Trouble*, as the title of this third volume, is to illustrate that no matter what you're going through, you are not alone.

A young boy was happily skipping through the park, enjoying life to its fullest. An elderly gentleman who sat on a park bench noticed and called out, "Young man, I'll give you a dime if you can tell me where God is." Immediately the young boy turned and replied, "And sir, I'll give you a dollar if you can tell me where God is not."

In two of his lowest moments, the Bible records, *"the LORD was with Joseph."* The first time was when Potiphar bought him. The second time was when he was falsely accused of rape and imprisoned (Genesis 39:2, 21).

There is nowhere you can go where God is not. He is with you in trouble. You can trust Him with your whole heart.

Foreword
by Phillip Harrelson

This volume that you are about to read is a small taste of looking over the shoulder of a workman who has mined out the great truth of Scripture from the Psalms. What is missing is the ability to see the blood, sweat, and even tears that goes into the weekly sermon preparation of a serious biblical expositor.

While you read the words on the page, the prayer, the concern, and the burden of the pastor for a local church is not as easily discerned. However, this is more than just a collection of words that will be read in book form or even on an electronic device, they are the mind and soul of a godly pastor who has a concern for his flock that God has called for him to serve. Good preaching is biblical preaching!

This book is a witness to good preaching and the church in Omaha is greatly blessed to have the work of Brother Powell. For those who are not preachers, let this book whet your appetite for a greater depth of hunger for the Word.

I pray this book will also be a tool that will wean you away from the sensational and entertaining preaching that seems to be regular fare for the day.

I pray this book will convict preachers and cause them to want to dig into the Word for themselves and feed the flock of God that he has called us to have the oversight of.

A portion of the genesis of the sermons that you will read here had some of their beginnings in the spring of 2016 when pastors Myron Powell, Douglas Walker, and myself had some very challenging conversations. We were and are still deeply concerned about the biblical illiteracy that is evident in the apostolic world. While there are several factors that are responsible for this, we all concluded that some of the fault lay at the feet of those who week in and week out preach the Word of God to their local congregations. For those of us called to preach, there needs to be a great priority placed on our task of prayer and ministry of the Word.

As you read through the sermons, may the voice of Brother Powell draw you closer to the voice of God!

A fellow workman,
Philip Harrelson
Pastor, The Pentecostals of Dothan
Dothan, Alabama

Table of Contents

Chapter 1	From the Mire to the Choir	1
Chapter 2	The Bread of Betrayal	9
Chapter 3	Hope in God, for I Shall Again Praise Him	17
Chapter 4	One Nation Under Siege	26
Chapter 5	A Royal Wedding Love Song	32
Chapter 6	The IS-ness of God	39
Chapter 7	Rejoicing in the Reign	47
Chapter 8	The Beautiful City of God	54
Chapter 9	Why Should I Fear in Times of Trouble	60
Chapter 10	Worthless Worship	69
Chapter 11	A Kingdom Alignment	78
Chapter 12	Planted in God's House	84
Chapter 13	The Fallacy of Atheism	90
Chapter 14	Behold! God is my Helper!	97
Chapter 15	But I Will Trust in You	103
Chapter 16	This I Know That God is for me!	112
Chapter 17	Be Exalted O God	117
Chapter 18	Surely There is a God who Judges the Earth	123
Chapter 19	Who Are You?	130
Chapter 20	The Transformation From Trouble to Triumph	137
Chapter 21	On Christ the Solid Rock I Stand	144
Chapter 22	You Are God Alone!	150
Epilogue	*by Paul Kinney*	157

From the Mire to the Choir
Psalm 40

Chapter 1

David found joy unspeakable and full of glory in the midst of one of the most difficult times of his life. God inspired David to record his experience for our encouragement in Psalm 40. We don't know what his difficult circumstances were, but they were emotionally painful. He compared his ordeal to a hole into which he had fallen.

Maybe it was the pit of rejection that seemed to engulf him. King Saul's jealous hatred led to a ruthless manhunt. He chased David from place to place and caused him to despair.

Perhaps it was a pit of family problems. David certainly knew trouble in his household, as his own son Absalom rebelled against him. Or possibly it was a pit of sin into which David had dug himself. Maybe it was a pit of loneliness in which David often found himself.

No matter how insignificant, David may have allowed his problems to be enlarged disproportionately in his own mind. Whatever the pit was, it was real to David. Yet, during this ordeal, David put his complete trust in God, calling upon the name of the LORD. The deliverance came, which then caused a new song to spring forth from David's heart.

He brought me out! (v.1-5)

The phrase *"I waited patiently"* means "waiting I waited." The Hebrew word from which this phrase is derived, does not imply a waiting to see if something will occur, but a waiting with the assurance that something will happen. It is waiting with expectation, trusting confidently in the Lord.

Waiting for God to help us is not easy, but David received four benefits from waiting: (1) God lifted him out of his despair, (2) God set his feet on solid ground, (3) God steadied him as he walked, and (4) God put a new song of praise in his mouth.

David testified that God lifted him out of the pit of destruction–distress so severe that he could not escape on his own. This trial is portrayed as a pit of mud and mire, representing a time in his life when he was trapped and could not escape.

Whatever the pit, God graciously intervened, rescuing David, raising him, and placing his feet on a rock. This gave him a firm place to stand. From the sinking sand of the pit, David was placed by the Lord on solid rock.

God also put a new song in his mouth, indicated by the abundant joy that flooded his heart. This new work of grace prompted a new hymn of praise. This singing by David was so open and unrestrained that he acclaimed many would see and fear the Lord who worked so wonderfully for his people. As a result of David's testimony, many would be encouraged to put their trust in the LORD.

You may not be a psalmist or songwriter like David, and you may not be in the church choir. But I would venture to say you could reach back into your past and testify of God helping you when you were in trouble. God brought you out to establish you!

As David considered God's goodness to him, he concluded, *"they are more than can be numbered."* He realized that God's goodness to him was far greater than he deserved. David could have tried to list all the things God did, but he would have needed all the paper in the world, and it still would have only scratched the surface of God's wondrous deeds.

The *"wonderful works"* are a reference to all the things God had done for David. So overwhelming is the mercy of God that David must declare, *"You have no equal"* (Psalm 40:5, New Living Translation).

"God brought you out to establish you!"

He filled me up! (v.6-8)

Although David lived about a thousand years before Jesus Christ would fulfill the Law, he understood that God wanted true relationship and worship and not just the burnt offerings and sacrifices of a religious practice.

Long before Jesus Christ would live, die, rise again, and pour out His Holy Spirit, David knew God wanted to put His *"law within my heart."*

Being about two thousand years after Calvary and Pentecost, I can testify that while God loved me where I was, He did not leave me where I was. God found me empty but filled me with unconditional love, illimitable mercy, joy unspeakable, and peace that passes all understanding.

David referred to his commitment to God being written *"in the volume of the book,"* which he had made probably at the time of his enthronement.

David was remembering and rededicating himself to keep God's commands. This written volume was most likely the scroll kings would write at their coronation that would be kept on one side of their throne. It was their personal commitment to God's Word and would serve alongside the Torah as their divine charter for governing the land. David had emptied himself in repentance, and God filled him up with His law.

Maybe the reason you're not full of God is you're still full of yourself. God doesn't want your religious practices. God wants relationship! That's what David is preaching to us here. David did not search the Torah to try and find loopholes; he studied the Torah to delight himself in the Lord.

> *"Maybe the reason you're not full of God is you're still full of yourself."*

He poured me out! (v.9-10)

In a poem titled The Chosen Vessel, Beulah V. Cornwall says, "There's work you must do, just pour out to others as I pour into you." The reason God filled you up was so He could pour you out!

> *"There's work you must do, just pour out to others as I pour into you."*

Since God's law fills David's heart (v.8), he is going to preach *"righteousness in the great congregation."* David knows he has been filled up to be poured out and is a willing vessel for God.

If you are a citizen of the United States of America, and are arrested, you will be told; "You have a right to remain silent. Anything you say to anyone can and will be used against you." And in a court of law, you could plead the 5th Amendment, further refusing to speak.

But, regardless of where you live on planet earth, if you are a born-again believer, you do not have a right to remain silent. Instead, you have a mandate from God to preach His righteousness, pouring out what He has poured into you.

God did not transform your life, heal your broken heart, forgive all your iniquities, and fill you with His Spirit so that you can be on display in a museum. God did all these things so that you can and will reveal Him to others.

Can I be so bold as to suggest that if you're unwilling to share your testimony–to be poured out –that, in essence, you're saying you don't care if others go to hell?

If I discovered the cure for all cancers, but chose to keep it a secret, how insensitive and cold-hearted would I be? I can imagine that every doctor in the world would do their best to get the antidote from me.

I do not have the antidote to cure every cancer, but I do know the Answer for every sin. I do know His blood atones for all sin. I do know that in one day His sacrifice took away all iniquity, past, present, and future. And I know the blood of Jesus Christ still flows today in the lives of those who request it of Him. I know that His salvation has been extended unto man by the death, burial, and resurrection of Jesus Christ.

And if you think I'm going to keep my mouth shut about it, you've lost your mind! I choose to pour out to others what God has poured into me! I don't want anyone to go to hell, and neither does God! It is not His will that any should perish but that all should come to repentance! Therefore, you'll have to cut out my tongue and cut off my head before I stop telling everyone I can about Jesus Christ and what He's done for me. Just like David, God took me from the mire to the choir, and He will do it for you.

Conclusion (v.11-17)

The underlying theme of this final portion of the text is summed up in verse 16. David opens this final stanza declaring what God has done for him and closes it explaining that God will do it for you.

The great salvation is not for a select few! Jesus Christ was the Lamb of God who took away the sin of the world. God can bring you out. He can fill you up! He can pour you out! He wants to do it again! He wants to do it for you!

Will you let God work in your life? Will you surrender and submit to God? Will you testify publicly of all God has done for you? God will take what's wrong and give you a song. Will you let Him do so for you?

The Bread of Betrayal
Psalm 41

Chapter 2

When we find ourselves *"in time of trouble,"* we should use Psalm 41 to take an inventory of our spiritual condition by asking and answering four questions: (1) how do we treat others?, (2) how do others treat us?, (3) how does God treat us?, and (4) how do we treat God?

In this psalm, David was at just such a point in his life. He was undergoing much adversity, and yet he was blessed. He was betrayed by a close friend, and yet he persevered. This psalm is a passionate prayer for God's mercy, and its central theme is that those who show mercy will receive mercy.

Psalm 41 reveals the contrast between those who show mercy to those in need, and those who deal treacherously with those in need. Those who are merciful are the ones whom God will deliver in their day of trouble.

Integrity–How do we treat others? (v.1-4)

Before we can claim God's promises, we must examine our hearts to see if we have sincerely met His terms. Do I treat people the way Jesus would treat them? Do I love as He loved, serve as He served, and give as He gave? We want God's promises, but there are no promises without first obeying God's precepts.

Who is the poor in your community that you consider? The word *"considereth"* means "to be circumspect, prudent, or wise." The word *"poor"* can be translated as weak, powerless, or insignificant depending on the context, but it does not automatically mean homeless and helpless. It can also mean those who are poor in spirit who need to hear the gospel.

The Bible also gives us these interactions regarding those who are poor in spirit in Ephesians 5:15-17 and Colossians 4:5-6. It's easy to overlook the poor. But the blessed man not only sees a poor man, a poor woman, or a poor family–he also takes time to consider or regard them.

It's more than compassionate concern; it is careful thought and reflection to know the right thing to do for the poor. Those who consider the poor do not just have warm feelings–they give the poor their time and attention to discover what truly needs to be done to help them (James 2:14-17).

The blessings God gave to David came to him because he confessed his sins and asked God to be merciful to him. It's important that we confess our sins to the Lord. Yet, if we have not been merciful to others, how can our heart be right to ask Him for mercy?

Treachery–How do they treat us? (v.5-9)

David's enemies spewed hatred and malice in their words and actions. They uttered their hurtful words, not caring about the emotional impact they would have on David.

David mentions *"enemies"* in verse 5, but his *"own familiar friend"* in verse 9. Who was this close friend whom David trusted, who shared bread with him, yet betrayed him? Was it Ahithophel who had served as a counselor to David but betrayed him when Absalom performed his coup of the throne? We may never know who David's familiar friend was, but we do know the emotional pain David endured because of this friend's betrayal.

Psalm 41:9 implicitly prophesies the betrayal of Judas, who would eat bread with Jesus, only to betray Him a few hours later.

Judas betrayed Jesus. Peter denied Jesus. But do you know that every other disciple deserted Jesus in Gethsemane that night, except for John? Only John would stay close and be at the foot of the cross with Him. But all of them would doubt; all of them would in one way or another deny Him. All of them ate the bread and betrayed Him in His moment of greatest trial. All of them would sleep instead of praying with Him in His final prayer meeting before His death.

And while it is easy to judge the disciples, how many times have I failed God? How many times have I denied, doubted, and deserted Him? How many times have I slept when I should have been praying? How many times have I robbed God, not giving my tithes and offerings? How many times have I mistreated one of His saints, not loving them as Christ loved them? How many times have I been unmerciful to others, although I have received mercy for my sin? How many times have I committed treachery against someone?

I have eaten the bread and then betrayed Jesus, and for that, I must repent, confess my sin, and renew my relationship with Him.

Mercy—How does God treat us? (v.10-12)

David does not respond to the accusations of his enemies, but wholeheartedly trusts in the LORD and in His promise to protect him. For in maligning the psalmist, David's enemies have maligned the God of Israel! Even in his adversity David is confident that the Lord will be true to his promises. Within his heart, David knows he is a man of integrity.

David prayed for mercy because he knew he had sinned (v.4). He also affirmed his integrity (v.12), for he had walked before the Lord in humility and submission.

When confronted with his sins, he confessed them and sought the face of the Lord. Many believed David's sickness to be a sign that God was against him. But he knew God was pleased with him. And since David had shown mercy to the weak (v.1) and confessed his sin (v.4), he could say to God, I know that you are pleased with me.

If, like David, you've repented and shown mercy, then remind yourself that God is for you. Remind yourself that God promises to never leave you nor forsake you. Remind yourself that in your weakness, you are made strong in and through Jesus Christ.

Returning to the prophetical connection to Judas, I must ask: Would Jesus have forgiven Judas? I believe the answer is yes. He called Judas, "friend," in the

Garden. And I believe since God delights in mercy, if Judas had come to Him repenting and confessing, Jesus would have forgiven him.

He forgave a thief who had just railed on Him. He forgave Peter who denied, Thomas who doubted, and the other disciples who deserted Him. Jesus forgave me.

I've eaten the bread and drunk the cup and have still sinned and come short of the glory of God. I don't say that to boast; rather, I say that with pain. But I've also found that when I repented, confessed, and forsook my sin, He gave me mercy and grace, neither of which I deserved.

Like David in this psalm, there have been many times I was blameless in the situation and was mistreated by others. But God has never mistreated me. He has never failed me. He has never forsaken me because He is *"not willing that any should perish, but that all should come to repentance"* (2 Peter 3:9).

I may not be able to explain God's mercy, but neither can I deny it. I cannot tell you why He extended mercy and grace, but I'm thankful He did.

> *"God has never mistreated me.*
> *He has never failed me.*
> *He has never forsaken me."*

Conclusion: How do we treat God? (v.13)

Psalm 41 is for anyone wanting to make a comeback. You may be broken, bruised, and betrayed, but you are still blessed because God is faithful to be merciful. You may have deserted Him, but you can follow Him again. You may have doubted Him, but He's standing next to you today. You may have denied Him, but He's ready to forgive.

Three of the Patriarchs, Abraham, Isaac, and Jacob lied, but that's not how they ended! Your story is not over either, and the last time I checked, God is still the Author and Finisher of your faith. If He hasn't put the pen down yet, then don't give up. Your life can bring blessing and glory to the LORD forever and ever!

You may have sinned yesterday, but at Midnight, there will be new mercies available. You may have a past riddled with denial and doubt; you may have deserted God, but you can make a comeback and be blessed beyond measure.

Eating a common meal together in Biblical times was more than just fellowship and food. The implications were deep, indicating close friendship and covenant relationships. Agreements and covenants were entered into as the parties involved would break bread together. The idea was that if we will eat together, we will be family throughout eternity.

    Each of the disciples who deserted Jesus was disgusted with himself for deserting Him. Thomas was upset that he doubted, and Peter was embarrassed that he denied. But each of these made a comeback. Like the prodigal son, they all returned to Jesus. They were not perfect, but they were forgiven. And each of them paid the ultimate sacrifice, being martyred for their faith in Jesus Christ.

    Reading of their martyrdom, one could wonder if they had thoughts of Jesus in their final moments. Did they hear His voice once more? Did they see Him praying in the Garden? Did they remember breaking bread with Him that final and fateful night He was betrayed?

    Whatever they may or may not have remembered, this we know, they had a comeback. They had partaken of the bread and cup over and over, showing the Lord's death. You, too, can make a comeback! You can eat the bread and drink the cup again.

"You can make a comeback and be blessed beyond measure."

Hope in God,
For I Shall Again Praise Him
Psalms 42 & 43

Chapter 3

The repeated refrain (42:5, 11; 43:5), and the general theme of these two psalms are why I am explaining them together in a single chapter. Another point of great interest is the superscription which states, *"To the chief Musician, Maschil, for the sons of Korah."* This marks the first psalm ascribed to someone other than David and raises the question, is this a wisdom psalm for the sons of Korah, or possibly written by the sons of Korah?

Korah, along with Dathan and Abiram, opposed Moses. They were not content to serve at the level of ministry God had called them to serve. They did not want to submit and serve; they wanted prestige and preeminence. A lesson everyone can learn from these three is that if you are too big to serve where there is a need, you are too small to lead where there is an opportunity.

Because of their sin, God judged them and their families, opening the ground and swallowing them alive. And the Bible is specific that their families were also judged. This parallels Achan, whose sin cost the life of his family as well as himself.

So, if the families of Korah were punished along with him, who are these *"sons of Korah"* that either write this and many other psalms, or are the subject of the psalms bearing their name?

Could it be there was a great-grandson of Korah that did not perish in God's punishment? There must have been. There had to have been. Could it also be possible then that generations after their great-grandfather's mistake, the sons of Korah have changed their family's legacy to a positive one?

"If you are too big to serve where there is a need, you are too small to lead where there is an opportunity."

Take note of all the psalms written to or by *"the sons of Korah"* and realize that no matter what your ancestors did, you can make a positive change in the outcome of your life. You do not have to be defined by their sin! In fact, if you are born again, you can lay claim to the heritage of your Heavenly Father.

If, in fact, the sons of Korah wrote under the inspiration of the Holy Ghost, telling us to, *"Hope thou in God, for I shall yet praise him,"* three times in the sixteen verses of Psalms 42 and 43, then you can have a testimony too! If they can change their family legacy, then you can change yours!

These two psalms show all believers how to overcome their bouts of depression. Psalms 42 and 43 describe the upward look of a downcast soul that has found peace by trusting in God.

Even the strongest believers can suffer extreme discouragement and despair. But let it be known that trust in God steadies the soul and brings peace. It is this faith in God during a time of discouragement that is expressed in Psalms 42 and 43.

In the face of mounting trials and painful agony, the sons of Korah rallied their own devastated heart to look to God. In this state of dependence on God, they found the comfort they needed. Although their discouragement was great, the hope they received in God was greater.

"Psalms 42 and 43 describe the upward look of a downcast soul that has found peace by trusting in God."

Maybe you are reading this and still think you're unworthy? Maybe you still think you are defined by your past? May I remind you of some others who could have made the same excuse?

Noah got drunk.
Abraham lied and was too old.
Jacob was arrogant and lied.
Moses was a murderer.
Gideon was afraid.
Rahab was a harlot.
Ruth was from the heathen nation of Moab.
Jeremiah and Timothy were too young.
Elijah and Job didn't want to live.
Jonah ran from God.
Peter denied Jesus.
Thomas doubted Jesus.
And all but John deserted Jesus.

Should we sin that grace abounds? God forbid! But neither should we define ourselves by our past or our parents' past! Satan looks at your past and proclaims, "You're not worthy." Jesus looks at His cross and declares, "So what; I AM!" *"Hope thou in*

God: for I shall yet praise him" needs to become the anthem of everyone reading this book!

Longing for God (42:1-5)

The sons of Korah open Psalm 42 with a desire for more of God. Comparing their desire to that of a deer that seeks to quench her thirst, these sons of Korah realize God is their source of life. And yet, it's obvious some people thought they shouldn't be allowed to be in the presence of God (v.3-5).

I'm quite certain these sons of Korah knew the painful history of their ancestors, and they didn't need anyone reminding them what their father had done.

And yet, although they remember and pour out their souls to God, this first section ends with a declaration of faith and confidence, *"Why are thou cast down, O my soul? and why are thou disquieted within me? hope thou in God: for I shall yet praise him, who is the health of my countenance, and my God.* Despite what others said or thought of them, they encouraged themselves in the Lord their God.

Others may think I'm unworthy and undeserving of God's presence. But my hope is not in my past or other's opinions of me; my hope is in God!

Peter failed when he denied that he knew Jesus, but when he saw Jesus on the shore, he did not wait for the others to finish pulling in the nets and row to shore—he dove in and swam as fast as he could because he longed for God.

Do you long for God? Then run to him regardless of what you've done or what others say.

> *"My hope is not in my past or other's opinions of me; my hope is in God!"*

Remembering God (42:6-11)

The emotional and spiritual landscape changes from a drought comparison in the first five verses to a storm comparison in the next six verses.

Sometimes even with encouraging yourself in the Lord, things still go from bad to worse. And although this is the case, the sons of Korah still proclaim God as their "Rock!" When your heart is overwhelmed, you can go to the Rock that is higher than you. When the storms rage against you, you can be steadfast, anchored to the Rock!

From verse 6, *"Mizar"* means "littleness." Maybe these sons of Korah felt very small amid that storm. Yet, instead of choosing to focus on what others were saying or give in to their emotions, they chose to remember God! And yet again, despite what others said about them and their fears, the sons of Korah ended with hope and praise.

It's easy to give in to fickle feelings. It's tempting to be led astray by emotions, but when all hell seems to be breaking loose against you, and it seems like all hope is lost, say these words with boldness; *"hope thou in God: for I shall yet praise him."*

Trusting God (43:1-5)

The sons of Korah revealed their longing for God in 42:1-5. They showed how they remembered God in 42:6-11, and now they express how they are trusting God in 43:1-5. They didn't take matters into their own hands, but they asked God to vindicate them. They did not trust in their own ability, but rather trusted in God's ability.

Yes, there was cause for concern, and yes, they even felt abandoned by God. But, despite their feeling of abandonment, they immediately respond with these words, *"O send out thy light and thy truth: let them lead me; let them bring me unto thy holy hill, and to thy tabernacles."*

God was their strength (43:2) and their exceeding joy (43:4). Therefore, they could worship God, trusting that He would deliver them.

> *"They did not trust in their own ability, but rather trusted in God's ability."*

Conclusion

Oswald Chambers wrote, "It is not our trust that keeps us, but the God in whom we trust who keeps us." Times of tribulation either make us or break us. That is, it either drives us closer to God, or it drives us further away from God. But no one remains the same through the experience of deep pain. It all depends upon where a person's faith rests. A time of adversity for the person whose trust is in the Lord becomes a session of increased dependency upon the Lord.

Hope leads the sons of Korah away from despair. Their hope is in their God, whom they praise and trust.

Hope is waiting for God to act. Hope focuses on God. Hope says, "You are my God," trusting the fulfillment of His promises, even when help seems far off. To hope means to wait upon God's perfect timing with a confident and strong trust in God about the future.

When surrounded by various troubles and discouragement, there is a simple but sure remedy for spiritual depression. The cure for the troubled soul is to hope in God exclusively, knowing that He will never fail (Zephaniah 3:5) and cannot lie (Titus 1:2). When you find yourself in difficult times, the solution is always the same, hope in God!

When faced with demanding circumstances, we should put our confidence and trust in the Lord. This may sound too simplistic in man's eyes, but it is, nevertheless, heaven's solution.

Lasting peace and genuine contentment are found in only one place, hope in God. We must discipline our minds and direct our wills to hope in God when tempted to dissolve into a pool of despair.

Hope in God.

Nothing else and no one else can pull us out of the depressing moments of life. Put your hope in God. Rather than focusing outwardly on the enemies who surround you, you must look upward to God.

"Hope says, "You are my God," trusting the fulfillment of His promises, even when help seems far off."

One Nation Under Siege
Psalm 44

Chapter 4

As you read the following, think of each of these national tragedies that awakened people to action.

The Holocaust.
Pearl Harbor.
John F. Kennedy and Dallas, Texas.
Martin Luther King and Memphis, Tennessee.
September 11, 2001.

Sometimes it is a foreign attack from the outside. Sometimes it's internal conflict from the inside. Such events can devastate people, but hopefully, people will seek the Lord for their strength and hope.

This was the situation in Psalm 44. It highlighted a national lament offered to God after Judah suffered a devastating defeat at the hands of a foreign oppressor. While the actual historical setting is uncertain, this much is known: Israel had enjoyed many victories in her past but found herself reeling under the devastating attacks of a military enemy, perhaps the Babylonian empire. So great were those losses that Judah suffered international ridicule.

The psalmist argued that these national defeats had happened undeservedly. He even asked God to point out the failure of their people, not expecting any to be revealed. The psalmist concluded Psalm 44 by calling on God to arise and deliver His people from their distress.

The Jewish people would sing praises to God after their great victories, but this psalm was sung after a humiliating defeat. Perhaps this psalm was used at a National Day of Prayer with the chief musician speaking the "*I/my*" verses and the people speaking the "*we/our*" verses.

Psalm 44 is a national lament reflecting defeat in battle. It is a Maschil psalm, meaning it is one that should be contemplated so that a lesson is learned. So, what can we learn from this psalm?

Israel's prosperous past (v.1-8)

Jewish parents were faithful to obey God and tell their children and grandchildren what the Lord had done. God's people were participants in the history of redemption. They had heard the story of what God had done for their ancestors in the days of old, including the era of the conquest. Against all odds, Israel inherited the land because God fought on behalf of his covenantal people. This type of in-home discipleship is seen as the sons of Korah began by referring to God's past victories on behalf of his people.

The emphasis in verses 2-3 lies on God's leadership and participation. That Yahweh had fought for them is expressed metaphorically as God's right hand and arm. Israel's victories were not their own. Though they used their swords and were valiant in battle, they realized that the fulfillment of the promise of land was God's. They were recipients of His favor.

Verses 4-8 begin with the emphatic confession, *"Thou art my King, O God."* Yahweh was the commander of Israel's army. The psalmist confessed his reliance on the Lord, stating he trusted in God, and not his weapons. Only when the Israelites had put aside their confidence in weaponry and bravery could they become instruments in the hands of God.

They fought and were victorious only through the One True God.

Israel's painful present (v.9-22)

Suddenly, the focus and tone of the psalm shift. Despite past victories, the nation was now subjected to devastating defeats. But the people were perplexed: if God gave them the land in His grace and enabled them to defeat their enemies, why was He now forsaking them and allowing the idolatrous nations to conquer them? It seemed that God had forsaken His people and abandoned His covenant. It was a dark day for the people of God, and they could not understand what He was accomplishing.

Whenever there was trouble in Israel, the first assumption was someone had sinned. But as far as the psalmist knew, there was no sin to be confessed because the people were faithful to the Lord. God could search their minds and hearts and not find any breach of the covenant.

They were faithful to God, they had not turned to the idols for help, and now they were giving their lives to protect the land that He had so graciously given them. Paul quoted verse 11 in Romans 8:36 as part of his magnificent argument that nothing could separate God's people from His love, not even defeat.

Psalm 44 is proof that sometimes while doing good, you still suffer bad things. This does not mean God hates you, or that you're not blessed and highly favored, or that you are cursed. Not all suffering is because of sin. Sometimes you suffer simply because you're a disciple of Christ.

"No situation is so bleak that it is beyond the redeeming power of God."

Israel's positive prospect (v.23-26)

Considering their dire predicaments, the psalmist called out to God to come to their aid. This psalm concludes with a passionate appeal for divine intervention to grant them victory over their enemies as he had done in previous days.

The questions of faith usually do not receive an answer! The reason for the purpose of suffering for the people of God finds no resolution in this psalm. There is neither despondency nor evidence of anger with God. The voice of collective and individual lament expresses the difficulty of suffering without cause. Trust looks to God for His deliverance regardless of the circumstance.

Conclusion

No matter how threatening a national tragedy may appear to be, there is always hope for the future as people put their trust in the Lord. The God who brought victory to Judah in the past, is the same God who can give victory in the present to those who call upon His name.

Even the cultural and societal upheavals that surround the righteous can be used by God to cause the hearts of people to seek Him. The people of God, like these ancient psalmists, should call upon God to redeem them from their nation's moral chaos. No situation is so bleak that it is beyond the redeeming power of God.

We can't always explain the tragedies of life, especially those that happen to God's people, but Romans 8:28 is still in the Bible, giving us hope that *"all things work together for good to them that love God, to them who are the called according to his purpose."*

Whether a national tragedy or a personal one, you can put your trust in God. Whether the answer comes today or tomorrow, you can put your trust in God. God is sovereign no matter what!

"There is always hope for the future as people put their trust in the Lord."

A Royal Wedding Love Song
Psalm 45

Chapter 5

Psalm 45 is a royal psalm and used as a love song at the occasion of the wedding of a royal couple. Yet, while this was used for those in the royal bloodline of David, this psalm points to a higher bloodline. This is a Messianic Psalm, pointing to the Marriage Supper of the Lamb, which is the second coming of Jesus Christ.

Psalm 45 serves as a reminder of God's responsibility to dispense justice and to bring order in the world. Psalm 45 gives the reader the inside scoop into what is happening in the palace as a reassurance that God cares.

The first institution that God established was marriage, an expression of His goodness to man. Beginning with the first wedding ceremony in Eden, each subsequent joining of a man and woman together in marriage is a celebration of God's blessing upon His creation. Psalm 45 reflects this divine goodness to man.

Unique among all the psalms, Psalm 45 is a song of praise to the king on his wedding day. Undoubtedly, this psalm was used during more than one royal wedding. It is a masterful piece of inspired literature that extols the joy and blessings of marriage.

In the New Living Translation, the inscription of Psalm 45 states it is *"a love song."* The King James Version adds that Psalm 45 is a *"Maschil"* intended to teach wisdom about the holy virtue of marriage.

"Psalm 45 gives the reader the inside scoop into what is happening in the palace as a reassurance that God cares."

It's quite possible you have been to a few weddings in your day. A few years ago, you may remember some were enamored with the British royal wedding of Prince Harry to Meghan.

But there is another royal wedding that is coming that I do not want to–indeed I cannot–miss! It is the catching away of the Bride of Christ, referred to as the *"marriage supper of the Lamb"* (Revelation 19:9).

So, whatever may have been the historical use of this psalm, its ultimate message is about Jesus Christ and His Bride, the Church.

The Royal Groom (v.1-7)

Jesus Christ will return! He came once to deal with sin, and He will come once more–this time to bring salvation to those who are eagerly looking for Him (Hebrews 9:28).

When Jesus came the first time, He was not handsome, as Psalm 45 portrays. Rather, Isaiah gives us a prophetical picture of what Christ looked like the first time He came. *"There was nothing beautiful or majestic about his appearance, nothing to attract us to him"* (Isaiah 53:2, New Living Translation).

When Jesus came the first time, He came to deal with sin. He came to be despised and rejected, to be hated and crucified, to take the chastisement of our peace, to take the stripes on His back to atone for our sin and reconcile us to Himself.

But the next time Jesus comes, He will not be coming to bring salvation. His sword girded on His thigh, He's coming with all His glory and majesty, and will eternally reward the righteous, but will pour out everlasting wrath on the wicked.

As the psalmist continues declaring the authority of the king, we again see prophetical overtones to the second coming of Jesus Christ: *"Thine arrows are sharp in the heart of the king's enemies."*

"Jesus Christ will return again!"

The radiant bride (v.8-12)

The descriptions in verse 8 speak of the radiant beauty of the bride and point to the Church, which is the body of Christ on the earth, and will be the bride of Christ in eternity.

We trade our sorrows for dancing, and our mourning for joy. We, who are baptized into Christ, have put on Christ, and are clothed with His righteousness and holiness—all of which are sweet smelling fragrances to God. We currently worship with all sorts of instruments, making us glad, and we are (and will be) seated in honor with Christ in heavenly places.

Like Ruth, we abandon Moab to devote ourselves and our loyalty to the One True God. This is what the psalmist describes in verse 10, *"forget also thine own people, and thy father's house."* And this indicates the bride was of foreign descent. She was not a native of Israel.

Just as Meghan was born and raised in the USA and is not a native of Great Britain, we were born in sin and shaped in iniquity. We were not born as natives of the kingdom of heaven.

When a Jewish man is betrothed to his future wife, upon her acceptance, she will go to a bathhouse where she will be completely submerged under water. Then, when she comes up out of the water, she will put on a new robe she has never worn before. And at this point, she can transact business in the name of her future husband.

Even though they have not consummated their marriage, she has pledged herself to her husband, as he has pledged himself to her. Because of this, she takes on his name and all the authority of it. Her betrothed will then say to her, "I will go and prepare a place for us and come again for you." She will then begin waiting and eagerly anticipating the day when he will return, and they will have their marriage ceremony.

And if this sounds familiar, it is because it is just like what happens when we repent and are baptized in the name of Jesus Christ for the remission of our sins. At that point, we put on Christ. When we receive the gift of the Holy Ghost, we speak with other tongues as the Spirit gives utterance and receive Christ in us, the hope of glory. And we then live with eager anticipation of the return of our Lord and Savior Jesus Christ.

The reward for identification with God's people and submission to the new way of life is exaltation among the nations (v.11). So, the young bride is comforted with words that bring out the advantages and honor of being a member of God's people and, more specifically, of the royal household.

As we submit to God, He delights in us, and we call Him Lord! Because we identify with Him, submitting to His holiness, we are exalted, comforted, and receive the benefits and honor of being in His kingdom.

The regal procession (v.13-15)

This royal wedding would include the most exquisite and regal procession. Everything about the bride is beautiful as she and her bridesmaids proceed to the palace. It would be a most joyous occasion as they enter the palace, and she is married to the king.

Imagine the most beautiful wedding you have ever seen. Next, add all the beauty Psalm 45 describes. Now, pick up your Bible and read Revelation 21 as God describes the regal beauty of His bride.

Can you see yourself rejoicing as you enter the throne room of the King of kings? What a day that will be!

The royal priesthood (v.16-17)

The royal priesthood alluded to in verses 16-17 is a perfect parallel to the church being a royal priesthood now (1 Peter 2:5, 9), as well as reigning with Christ as royal priests in His everlasting kingdom (Revelation 20:6).

Conclusion

Jesus Christ is coming soon. Are you ready to go when He comes? And when he comes, it will be a royal wedding love song for the redeemed. I want to be in that number and don't want to be like those recorded in Luke's gospel (Luke 21:23-28).

Scripture instructs us to make our calling and election sure. Jesus said we must be born again of water and the Spirit to both see and enter the kingdom of Heaven (John 3:3-8). Are you ready to go when Jesus comes?

The Is-ness of God
Psalm 46

Chapter 6

God is in trouble (v.1), God is in our midst (v.5), and God is with us (v.7, 11). Each of these should evoke rapturous praise. But you could also simply shorten each of these to say, "God is." God exists.

Psalm 46 is a song of Zion celebrating the presence of God. He is "for us" and "with us." God's people need not fear in the presence of the Great King, as the threefold repetition "for us" and the twofold repetition, "with us," assures them that God exists and cares for His own.

The emphasis of Psalm 46 is on the presence of the Lord with His people (v.1, 5, 7, 11) and the difference it makes when we trust Him in the challenges and difficulties of life. The psalm focuses on the Lord and both who and what He is to His trusting people.

> *"God is in trouble."*

God is in trouble (v.1-3)

I know it almost sounds sacrilegious to say, "God is in trouble," but it's true. Read Psalm 46:1 again, "**God is** *our refuge and strength, a very present help* **in trouble**." Did you notice the first two and last two words? The writer of the 91st Psalm agrees as he writes what the Almighty says, *"He shall call upon me, and I will answer him:* **I will be with him in trouble**; *I will deliver him, and honour him."*

While the specific trouble the psalmist writes about is unknown, the words are timeless, extending to us today. Our God is *"our refuge and strength."* God is our shelter from the storm. He protects us from danger. Our God is *"a very present help"* to His people. His help is exceedingly and abundantly on time, every time.

Something unique happens as the second verse begins and continues through the rest of the psalm.

Every phrase can be cross-referenced with apocalyptic prophetic passages. Therefore, Psalm 46 reveals the truth of Jesus Christ's second coming.

Verses 2 and 3 speak of the earth being removed, mountains floating out to sea, tsunami waves, and volcanoes, and the righteous witnessing it all but being divinely protected.

Going through trials and tribulation yet having God with you to be your refuge and strength, is a Biblical concept seen in both Old and New Testaments.

Joseph was sold to Potiphar and later cast into prison falsely accused, but in both instances, *"the LORD was with Joseph"* (Genesis 39:2, 21).

David said in Psalm 23:4, *"Yea, though I walk through the valley of the shadow of death, I will fear no evil: for thou art with me; thy rod and thy staff they comfort me."* David wasn't delivered out of the valley of the shadow of death; instead, God walked with him through it.

Writing explicitly of the imminent judgment of God on Nineveh, yet implicitly referring to the tribulation, Nahum sandwiches the protection of God in between two verses of apocalyptic judgment (Nahum 1:6-8).

When Jesus prayed for His disciples, a part of that prayer was, *"I pray not that thou shouldest take them out of the world, but that thou shouldest keep them from the evil."* The word *"keep"* means "to guard or attend to carefully; to take care of."

Each of these example's points to God being with His people through every trial and even through the Great Tribulation. When asked by His disciples, *"when shall these things be? and what shall be the sign of thy coming, and of the end of the world?"* (Matthew 24:3), Jesus warns against deception and speaks of *"the beginning of sorrows."* As He continued answering their questions, Jesus eventually told us when His second coming (Hebrews 9:28) would occur: *"Immediately after the tribulation...and then shall appear the sign of the Son of Man in heaven...and he shall send his angels with a great sound of a trumpet, and they shall gather his elect..."* (Matthew 24: 29-31). Jesus Christ is coming again after the tribulation to rapture the righteous and pour out His wrath on the wicked.

If you are born again, God promises to be with you now through every trial you encounter. And God also promises to be with you all the way to the end. If your end is death before the rapture, God will be with you. If you endure to the end of the tribulation, God will be with you. God is your *"very present help in trouble."*

> *"Jesus Christ is coming again after the tribulation."*

God is in our midst (v.4-7)

The *"city of God"* in verse 4 is a reference to the Church. It is this same city that Abraham searched for (Hebrews 11:10). It is the same city that John described in glorious detail as the Bride of Christ (Revelation 21:1-2, 9-10). And *"the river,"* whose streams make glad the Church, is the river of living water that springs up within those who are born again of the water and of the Spirit (John 7:37-39).

God is in the midst of His Church! No longer does He dwell in temples made with hands. No longer is worship confined to a single temple, in a single city, and on a single mountain. God dwells in His Church. And since God indwells His Church, nothing can cause her to be destroyed. This is further proven in Hebrews 12:25-29, reminding us that when the earth, the heavens, and the wicked shake and are destroyed at the coming of the Lord, we have received *"a kingdom which cannot be moved."*

All the military power in the whole world will be like a bug flying into a windshield. God might get a little blood on His garments, but at His Word, the earth will melt, and the wicked will be destroyed. Yet, during this chaotic and apocalyptic worldwide destruction, *"The LORD of hosts is with us; the God of Jacob is our refuge. Selah."*

God is exalted (v.8-11)

Simultaneously, as God pours out His wrath on the wicked, He will be resurrecting the righteous. We will meet Him in the clouds, along with those who have died in Christ, and will witness *"the works of the LORD, what desolations he hath made in the earth."*

The final battle, Armageddon, will also be the final war, as God causes them to cease! His fiery wrath will consume all the arsenals of the world's weapons, destroying them forever.

And then, all the earth will know that Jesus Christ is the Almighty God! He will be exalted, as every knee will bow, and every tongue will confess that He is Lord. (Romans 14:11; Philippians 2:20-11; Revelation 1:7-8).

The psalmist is inspired to repeat verse 7 verbatim in verse 11, reminding us that *"The LORD of hosts is with us; the God of Jacob is our refuge. Selah."* He first uses a name for God, indicating that He is the Commander of Heaven's Armies (*LORD of hosts*). He secondly uses a name for God, reminding us that He can change us from a liar to a prince (*God of Jacob*). This second name points to our new birth, being saved from the penalty of our sin.

Conclusion

The world is in trouble. Sin is paraded and applauded by celebrities and politicians. Churches have compromised the gospel to fill empty chairs. But all of these have forgotten that God is in trouble.

Think of the formless, empty expanse of darkness that existed just prior to God creating the world. God did not shy away from the chaos and confusion, but rather began moving and then spoke words of life and light that forever changed everything.

Now, compare that same formless void of nothing but darkness to the sin of the world. The same Spirit of God is still moving, and the same Word of God is still being spoken. Enticing words of man's wisdom are impotent! But a demonstration of the Spirit and power of God will transform lives eternally.

Tell me how dark and bleak and troubling your situation is, and I'll tell how powerful the eternal light of God's Word is! God is in trouble! Tell me how much sin abounds and I'll tell you God's grace abounds more! Tell me all about the enemy and I'll tell you, *"Greater is he that is in you, than he that is in the world"* (1 John 4:4).

Since we know God is with us from the beginning and will be with us through to the end, let us be encouraged that He is with us now! God is not disturbed by the political chaos. God is not shaken by financial crisis. God is not shying away from the atheistic and humanistic messages being spread abroad. God is in trouble!

This also means when the great tribulation begins, God will still be in trouble with His Church.

"Therefore we will not fear" (Psalm 46:2).

Rejoicing in the Reign
Psalm 47

Chapter 7

The Lord our God is the Unrivaled Sovereign over everything, ruling all nations and peoples, for His purposes. This position of supremacy should cause all His people to rejoice, offering praise to Him who presides over everything. This triumphant theme is the subject of this psalm. It is a dramatic declaration of the kingship of God over everything.

Every person is under God's rule, whether they acknowledge it or not. This is the essence of the message that is to be declared to the nations of the earth. God is the sole sovereign! He alone is God, possessing absolute authority and reigning in the heavens. Here is the reason for the people of God to rejoice: God reigns over all the earth (v.2, 7), the nations (v.3, 8), all peoples (v.3), Israel (v.4, 9), enemies (v.5), nobles (v.9), and kings (v.9). Every person is under the sovereignty of Almighty God.

The promise of Psalm 46:10– *"I will be exalted among the heathen, I will be exalted in the earth,"* is fulfilled in Psalm 47. Psalm 47 is used in the synagogues in Rosh Hashanah, the Jewish New Year's Day, and in the church to celebrate the Ascension of Jesus Christ.

This also makes it a Messianic psalm, with an emphasis on the coming kingdom. We who are born again–the Israel of God–can rejoice in the reign of Jesus Christ.

Elvis Presley was the king of rock-n-roll but lived and died. Michael Jackson was the king of pop but lived and died. James Brown was the king of soul but lived and died. But Jesus Christ, the King of kings, died and is alive forevermore (Revelation 1:18)! And that makes me want to shout!

> *"The Lord our God is the Unrivaled Sovereign over everything."*

Shout to God (v.1-4)

The opening call to worship, *"O clap your hands, all ye people; shout unto God with the voice of triumph,"* is universal, extending to everyone. What follows is why God should be so fervently worshipped.

Since the theme of this psalm is the kingship of the Lord, they worshipped Him the way they welcomed a new king. The early church patterned its worship after the synagogue and emphasized prayer, the reading and expounding of Scripture, and the singing of psalms, hymns, and spiritual songs. When Jewish people clapped their hands and shouted, it was to the Lord in response to His marvelous works.

They did not do it to praise the people who participated in the worship service. The people were struck with awe on account of the mighty works of the great King. Here, the emphasis is on God, who is *"the LORD Most High...the great King over all the earth."* God is the one who subdues enemies, giving His chosen people an inheritance, and is therefore worthy of shouts of exuberant praise!

Sing to God (v.5-7)

"Sing praises" is spoken four times in verse 6 and once in verse 7. This phrase acts as a repetitious call for God's people to give glory to the victorious God.

The reason for this boisterous worship is clear; *"For God is the King of all the earth."* God alone is worthy of our praise because He alone reigns over everything.

God fills heaven and earth, but when He acts on earth on behalf of His people, the Scriptures sometimes describe Him as coming down. He came down to visit the tower of Babel and judged the people building it (Genesis 11:5), and He also came down to investigate the wicked city of Sodom and destroyed it (Genesis 18:21). The night 185,000 Assyrian soldiers were slain by the angel, God came down bringing judgment (Isaiah 37:28-29, 36) and then went up in great glory to His holy throne (v.8).

But in this psalm, *"God has gone up with a shout,"* meaning He has ascended to His throne to judge the matter. And since He is the Righteous Judge, He will give true judgment. He cannot be bribed and will never give unfair judgment.

Some scholars believe this could also be a reference to rejoicing when the Ark of the Covenant returned, describing the presence of God reigning over Israel. Either way, this psalm prophetically points to the great Day of the Lord when He will reign over the earth.

"God alone is worthy of our praise because He alone reigns over everything."

Serve God (v.8-9)

God sits on the throne of His holiness, executing His sovereign will and doing as He pleases. Sitting does not imply laziness, but rather signifies God's righteous rule and reign. This same image is seen in Psalm 2, revealing that God sits and laughs at the wicked who think they can overrule or stop Him.

Verse 9 points to the Day of the Lord when all the world, and its leaders, will assemble before God's throne to acknowledge His Kingship. Interestingly, the psalmist writes, *"even the people of the God of Abraham,"* indicating that Jew, and Gentile alike, will be gathered together as one, and will declare God's sovereign Lordship. This points to the second coming of Jesus Christ when He will put an end to all forms of government and reign supreme.

Many world leaders and the empires they ruled over, have desired world dominance. From Alexander the Great to Hitler, all these godless leaders have failed. They have all died and will be resurrected to judgment before God.

Many nations have tried varying forms of man-made government. From despotism to dictatorship, from communism to socialism, and from being a republic to democracy, each of these has failed. But, when God reigns, His reign and government will be perfect and pure, for *"he is greatly exalted."*

Conclusion

Ultimately, this psalm looks ahead to God's rule through Christ over all the earth during the millennium (Revelation 20). In that glorious day, Christ will inaugurate His earthly reign, over all the nations, immediately following the time of His second coming (Revelation 19:15).

Triumphantly, the kingdoms of this world will become the kingdoms of our Lord (Revelation 11:15). When that climactic time comes for Christ to establish His kingdom upon the earth, He will descend from heaven and make His grand ascent to His throne as the unrivaled King of kings and Lord of lords. And every knee will bow, and every tongue will confess that Jesus Christ is Lord.

In the face of the present uncertainties and international crises, we can rejoice that God reigns on high and is soon to return to this earth to inaugurate His everlasting kingdom.

How can we ensure that we will rejoice in the reign of Christ? How can we make our calling and election sure so that we reign with Christ? Read John 3:3-8 and Acts 2:37-39 for the answer.

You can repent; you can be baptized in the name of Jesus Christ. You can be filled with the Holy Spirit and speak with other tongues as the Spirit gives you the utterance. You can rejoice in the reign of Jesus

Christ both now and throughout all eternity. Those who are born again have a blessed hope—the glorious appearing of our Lord and Savior Jesus Christ (Titus 2:11-14).

I choose to rejoice in His reign now and look forward to rejoicing in His eternal reign when He comes back.

> *"Triumphantly, the kingdoms of this world will become the kingdoms of our Lord."*

The Beautiful City of God
Psalm 48

Chapter 8

God is the LORD of all, the Great King of the universe. He is sovereign, powerful, and glorious, and He alone is worthy of the praise of all creation and all human beings. But God's people, citizens of the beautiful *"city of our God,"* have additional reasons for praising Him. These reasons are revealed throughout Psalm 48, namely, His presence, protection, love, and righteousness.

Our Great King has chosen to reside among His people in the city which is on the holy mountain. Remember, God dwells in the praises of His people!

Psalm 48 is a hymn of celebration, which focuses upon God's activity in this beautiful and holy city. God is in the midst of her, and she will not be shaken nor defeated by enemies.

Elevated joy (v.1-3)

The greatness of the city of God, Jerusalem, can be explained only by the greatness of God. Elevated above the surrounding terrain, Jerusalem was beautiful in its loftiness. As the joy of the whole earth, it was admired by other nations. And it still is today. Often it is called the international capital of the world. I was personally amazed at the beauty of Jerusalem when I saw it firsthand on a trip in 2018.

Because God was in Jerusalem's citadels, unusually present within her, He was her fortress. God was her high and safe place from her enemies. This means God Himself, not her exterior walls, was Jerusalem's true defense. The strength of her citadels and her fortress was the presence of God within her walls, not chariots or horses, ramparts, or towers.

David brought the ark of the covenant to Jerusalem, and this made Zion a holy mountain, for the Lord dwelt there. Jerusalem thus became *"the city of our God"* and *"the city of the great King."*

"God Himself, not her exterior walls, was Jerusalem's true defense."

Established forever (v.4-8)

God's protection of the city symbolizes the many ways in which He protects his people. Every act of unfailing love and righteousness spreads the fame of God's holy name.

The bold, confident, and strong opposition against God was broken miraculously. It is likened to the destruction of the "ships of Tarshish," which were the pride and glory of seafaring nations such as Phoenicia (v.7). How strong and majestic they were!

But how easily a strong wind could toss them about on the open sea and destroy the vessels, people, and cargo! The storming of the nation's came to an end as though destroyed by a stormy wind ordained by the Lord. The ease with which the Lord repels and destroys the opposition terrifies the nations.

Endless Praise (v.9-11)

The godly meditated upon God's mighty acts. Their meditation was more than a devotional reading. They took comfort in, rejoiced in, and made offerings in gratitude to the revelation of God's perfections. It was a God-given visual aid encouraging them to imagine, and to reflect upon the long history of God's involvement with Israel, and which served as evidence of His unfailing love.

The reaction of praise is a positive response in contrast to the dread that fell on the nations. To the ends of the earth, the praise of God is heard from the lips of the godly. They declare his righteousness, His victorious and glorious rule. The rule of God is symbolized by the right hand, which implies His power, justice, righteousness, and love.

Rejoicing goes from Mount Zion throughout Judah. The people rejoice in the judgments of God, and in the ways in which He established His kingdom by bringing defeat to the opposing forces.

Empowered discipleship (v.12-14)

Take notice in the last three verses of the detail at which they were to examine and explain Zion to the next generation. This is exactly what is meant by Deuteronomy 6, which should be our anthem as we practice discipleship. They were to trust in their God forever and ever, knowing He is the Good Shepherd!

Conclusion

But is this psalm referring to the geographical Jerusalem in Israel? Does Psalm 48 imply the

Israelites and the Mosaic Law? The answer to these questions is, "No." Just as the Law was a shadow of things to come, so also Jerusalem, with her Temple, is a shadow of things to come.

While the ancient "city of David" was a place where God's presence rested and reigned, God never intended to be confined to a single city, nor to a physical temple behind a veil. God's purpose all along was His Church. And those men and women of faith mentioned in Hebrews 11 searched for this very church. They wanted to see the promised fulfillment of the Messiah and His church. (Hebrews 11:10, 16; 12:10; 13:14).

The city Abraham and the other heroes of faith sought for was not the geographical city of Jerusalem. God was not the *"builder and maker"* of Jerusalem, but He is the builder and maker of His church (Matthew 16:18). These heroes of faith in Hebrews 11 were searching for the promise of the Church; they were searching for the Israel of God. Furthermore, Jesus Christ calls His Church *"a city that is set on an hill"* (Matthew 5:14).

So, if God thinks this much of His Church to compare her to the time when David put God first in the city of Jerusalem, and if God thinks this much of His Church to declare her beauty in both Old and New Testaments, then how much more should we love, respect, and tell others about God's Church, *"the city of the great King"*?

There is only one way to enter this beautiful city of God. To enter God's kingdom, you must be born again of the water and of the Spirit (John 3:5).

John prophesied of *"the city of the great King,"* calling her the Bride of Christ (Revelation 21). You can be a part of the Bride of Christ by being born again (John 3:5; Acts 2:38).

Why Should I Fear in Times of Trouble?
Psalm 49

Chapter 9

Psalm 49 has a message for everybody in the world. The important people and the nobodies, the rich and the poor (v.1-2). The psalmist speaks from his heart, the wisdom and understanding that the Lord gave him (v.3), and he deals with an enigma that only the Lord could explain, which is the puzzling conundrum of how some believe their wealth grants them special status, as well as power and prestige.

How do we respond when we see the rich get richer? Should we be afraid that the wealthy will abuse the poor? Should we be impressed by the wealth that others possess and seek to imitate them? What of the corruption associated with so many who are wealthy?

Psalm 49 gives us three reminders to help us keep our perspective in a world obsessed with wealth and the alleged yet temporal power it brings. In fact, this is the theme of this song which stands as a sharp and direct warning to all who put their trust in riches.

The psalmist counseled the godly not to envy the wicked in their prosperity or be seduced by their possessions, for the wicked will suffer destruction. Instead, the godly should live for God, and desire to abide in the new heavens and new earth, where true and eternal riches are found.

Psalm 49 is an encouragement to the godly who are haunted by the power and influence of the rich. The prosperity of the wicked is difficult to understand for some, but the psalmist has given a ray of light as to the final resolution. He does this by writing this wisdom psalm for posterity. His method includes questions, observations of life, proverbial conclusions, metaphors, and personification. All of which leads to wisdom while pointing out the folly of trusting in wealth.

Wealth cannot prevent death (v.1-12)

It is not a sin to be wealthy, so long as we acknowledge God as the Supreme Provider and use what He gives to help others and glorify His name, seeking Him first (Matthew 6:33; 1 Timothy 6:7-10). An increase in wealth often leads to an increase in evil. It's good to have things that money can buy if we don't lose the things money cannot buy. It's tragic when people esteem the acquisition of wealth over the development of moral values.

> *"It is not a sin to be wealthy."*

The psalmist feared that the wealthy in the land would start to take advantage of poor people. It was easy for the rich man to bribe judges and rob the poor of their rights.

Spencer W. Kimball wisely said, "Love people, not things; use things, not people." Sadly, many have this backwards! Those who boast of their wealth have a false sense of security, because their wealth can't protect them from the last enemy, which is death (1 Corinthians 15:26).

Jesus had this truth in mind when He spoke about the rich farmer in Luke 12:13-21. If a relative was poor, a Jew could redeem him by paying for his debts. But if a relative was dying, no amount of money could come to his rescue; besides, to whom would you give the money?

So, money can't rescue you on this side of the grave, nor can it rescue you on the other side of the grave, because you can't take your money with you. Whether you are rich or poor, wise or foolish, you leave everything behind.

Many wealthy people think they will go on forever and enjoy their houses and lands, only to discover that death is a great equalizer. For after death, the rich and the poor stand equal before God.

The greatest fool is the person who lives for the pursuit of riches in this world, only to lose his soul eternally. The rich may appear to be content, but their prosperity is only temporary. Death is approaching for everyone, and the grave is not prejudice.

Departure from this world will remove all our possessions, never to be enjoyed again. So why live to acquire temporal things which are not eternal? The greatest treasure of all is to possess what lasts forever and truly satisfies—eternal life!

Only those who are born again of the water and the Spirit will have true riches in this life. Furthermore, only they will be redeemed from death to live forever with God. This is what Jim Elliott had in mind when he said, "He is no fool who gives what he cannot keep; to gain what he cannot lose."

Psalm 49 stands as a warning to all who put their trust in riches. Don't envy the wicked in their prosperity or be seduced by their possessions, for they will suffer eternal destruction. Instead, live for God now so that you will one day enjoy eternity with Him: this is true wealth!

Godly wisdom gives prudence, insight, and discretion to its students. Wealth cannot ransom the life of another and provide escape from death. Only God can redeem your soul.

Life is such a costly commodity that it cannot be purchased. No payment, even from the wealthiest man, is ever enough to deliver from the certain destiny of death and decay. Death is no respecter of persons. All will leave their wealth to others when they die.

Earthly wealth cannot prevent death, but if you have laid up treasures in heaven, you will live eternally in the wealthiest of all places.

Wealth will not determine your destiny (v.13-15)

When Jesus told His disciples that it was hard for a rich person to enter the kingdom of heaven, they were astonished; for most Jews believed that the possession of wealth was a mark of God's blessing.

People with wealth tend to trust themselves and their money, believing the nice things people say about them (v.13). Yet, Psalm 49 depicts the wealthy as lost sheep being led to the slaughterhouse in death.

But for the born-again believer, death is only a valley of temporary shadows, and Jesus is their shepherd (23:4)! There is coming a morning when the dead in Christ will be raised and share the glory of the Lord (1 Thessalonians 4:13-18; Psalms 16:10-11; Isaiah 26:19; Daniel 12:3).

We can't ransom someone who is about to die (v.7-8), but the Lord has already ransomed us from sin and the power of the grave. New life in Christ, not the possession of great wealth, determines our eternal destiny!

The prideful trust in themselves and their wealth, but it is folly (v.13). Their fate will be like that of sheep being led to the grave. But the righteous will ultimately triumph over the wicked, obtaining eternal life beyond the grave. Whether you are wealthy or impoverished, obedience to God's Word alone determines your eternal destiny (1 John 2:17).

Wealth must not increase your desires (v.16-20)

Do not be impressed when you see others getting wealthy and buying bigger houses and cars. All their wealth will be left behind when they die and will ultimately lose its value in eternity. Remember; you take nothing with you when you die. (Job 1:21; Ecclesiastes 5:14; 1 Timothy 6:7).

If we have been faithful stewards of what God has given us, we possess eternal riches that will never fade (Matthew 6:19-34). You can't take wealth with you, but you can send it ahead! Through the faithful giving of your tithes and offerings, you are enabling the church to share the gospel locally, regionally, and globally.

The statement in verse 12 is repeated in verse 20 with the addition of the phrase *"and understandeth not."* Wealth cannot prevent death or determine your destiny, so you must not become covetous when you see others prospering in this world. Why envy the temporal trappings of a meaningless life? After death, the wealthy who trusted in their riches *"shall never see light."*

It isn't a sin to have wealth, provided you've earned it honestly, spend it wisely, and invest it faithfully in that which pleases the Lord Jesus Christ!

Because the wicked would perish despite their wealth, the godly must not let the prosperity of the rich captivate their hearts.

> *"You can't take wealth with you, but you can send it ahead!"*

Ending this psalm with dramatic bluntness, the psalmist describes a person who has riches in the world, yet does not understand spiritual truths about God, eternity, and redemption.

The fleeting pleasures of worldly riches are seductive and deceptive, able to pull people away from God. Instead of being duped and defrauded, the righteous must look to God for true satisfaction.

Jesus reasoned, *"For what is a man profited, if he shall gain the whole world, and lose his own soul? or what shall a man give in exchange for his soul?"* (Matthew 16:26). The implied answer is obvious.

Conclusion

This wisdom psalm reminds us of the book of Ecclesiastes with its emphasis on the futility of worldliness. But unlike Ecclesiastes, Psalm 49 brings out the assurance of victory over death for the righteous.

While we are surrounded by those who trust in their wealth and use it to bribe, deceive, and seemingly get away with all sorts of sin against God, the wise answers found in Psalm 49 give and bring hope.

Although death comes to all, only those who are righteous—those who are born again and have laid up treasure in heaven—will triumph in the end.

No matter how much deprivation and oppression you've seen in this life, or how much you've been scorned and hounded by those with money and power, there is a day of reckoning coming, and the righteous have been promised something far better than vain, temporal wealth.

The man God called a fool was the man who built bigger barns. He wasn't a fool because he built barns; he was a fool because he only lived for this life. Live for Jesus Christ while on this earth, so that you may enjoy eternity with Him. Store up treasures in heaven where moth, rust, and thieves cannot steal, kill, or destroy it.

Worthless Worship
Psalm 50

Chapter 10

Every seventh year, during the Feast of Tabernacles, the priests were obligated to read the Law to the people and explain its meaning. Psalm 50 may have been written for such an occasion. The emphasis is on the consistent godly living that should result from true, spiritual worship.

Asaph, a music minister, is the writer of Psalm 50, and he uses language depicting a court scene to reveal God's message. God the Judge summons the court (v.1-6) and confronts two offenders: the formalist, to whom worship is a ritual to follow (v.7-15), and the hypocrite, to whom worship is a disguise to cover sin (v.16-21). The closing arguments call all worshippers to be faithful to God (v.22-23).

There are times when worship may seem by all outward appearances to be proper and acceptable, even skilled, and beautiful. But as God observes it, He sees it for what it really is.

Half-hearted, apathetic praise is an abomination to God. Such worthless worship flows from external ritual and empty routine and is devoid of genuine relationship. God detests such meaningless activity because the heart of such worshippers is far from Him. (Matthew 15:7-9). Instead of the vain worship Israel gave, God seeks true worship (John 4:23-24).

Psalm 50 provides insight into those times when worship is wrong. The courtroom setting is represented, in which God summons His people to appear before Him to answer for their lukewarm worship. He condemns them for approaching Him with self-sufficient attitudes, devoid of thanksgiving. And God rejects such worthless worship.

Psalm 50 is prophetic and pointed, calling the people of God to fervent and focused worship.

> *"Half-hearted, apathetic praise is an abomination to God."*

The Holy Judge (v.1-6)

God is The Honorable Judge, as well as the Prosecutor and Jury. He knows all about those who are on trial and calls heaven and earth to witness the proceedings.

The appearance of a human judge entering a courtroom is accompanied by a show of respect. God's entrance into the assembly is accompanied by the shining of His glory and a fiery tempest, not unlike the scene at Mount Sinai when He gave His Law. When we forget the transcendence of God, we find it easier to sin. Yet the opposite is also true. The more submitted to God that we are, the less value this world will have for us.

Some of God's people had sinned, and God had been long-suffering with them and even silent about the matter. They interpreted His silence as consent, but now the time had come for God to speak. The purpose of this trial was not to judge and condemn the sinners, but to expose their sins and give them an opportunity to repent and return to the Lord.

God's rule extends far beyond Israel to the whole earth, poetically described as *"from the rising of the sun unto the going down thereof."* God, the Righteous Judge, will order everything on earth in accordance with His will. He does not tolerate anything that does not satisfactorily meet His requirements.

"The more submitted to God that we are, the less value this world will have for us."

The heartless worshipper (v.7-15)

God addresses those people of His whose hearts are not truly worshipful. Although they are faithful in their devotion, the routine way they conduct themselves is not from a sincere heart. Like the church at Ephesus, they had *"left their first love"* and were worshipping the Lord out of habit rather than from the heart.

Outwardly, they were doing what the Lord commanded and were honoring the daily sacrifices, but inwardly they lacked love and fellowship with God. They forgot that God wanted their hearts before He wanted their sacrifices. God wanted them to rend their hearts, not their garments (Joel 2:13).

The sacrifices that the Lord commanded were indeed important to the spiritual life of the nation of Israel, but they did not do any good for the worshippers, unless there was faith in their hearts and a desire to honor the Lord. The animals they brought belonged to Him long before the worshippers ever saw them. The world and everything in it belong to Him. So, what can we truly give Him except true worship (John 4:23-24)?

What the Lord wanted from His people was thanksgiving from their hearts, obedience to His Word, authentic prayer, and a true fear of Him in everything (v.14-15). God does not want ritualism or formalism; He wants our worship to come from the heart (Joel 2:13; John 4:23-24).

God does not need or want offerings, not even dedicatory offerings, if they do not express true gratitude and joy from the hearts of the givers. To this end, He reminds the people that He is the Creator-Ruler, and everything belongs to Him (v.9-12).

He does not need the few animals the Israelites have presented with a sense of pride and obligation. What are the tens of thousands of animals from Israel's stalls and pens compared with the hills and mountains that already belong to Him?

While Israel was arrogantly boasting of their offerings from their homes, God replied to their pride by stating emphatically, *"If I were hungry, I would not tell thee: for the world is mine, and the fulness thereof."*

The significance of the offerings was in the people's attitude of the heart. The offerings and vows were to be concrete expressions of gratitude and dedication to The Most High God. When the spirit of pride is broken, and their trust in God is restored, they will again enjoy the benefits of answered prayer and experience the Lord's deliverance of those who call on Him. In response, they are expected to give honor to God with heartfelt joy.

The hypocritical sinner (v.16-21)

Verses 16-21 were addressed to *"the wicked."* These were the Israelites in the covenant community who were reciting the creed with their lips but were also deliberately disobeying God's law. Brennan Manning's quote describes this hypocrisy:

> "The greatest single cause of atheism in the world today is Christians who acknowledge Jesus with their lips and walk out the door and deny Him by their lifestyle. That is what an unbelieving world simply finds unbelievable."

After breaking God's Law, these wicked Israelites would go to the sanctuary and act very religiously so they could cover up their sins. By their proud actions, they made the sanctuary a den of thieves.

They had no respect for God's Word (v.17) and not only consented to the sins of others but participated in them and enjoyed doing so (v.18-20). They hated instruction, rejecting God's way of life. They rejected God's Word and lived irresponsibly and immorally.

The psalmist mentions stealing, adultery, and slander, three of the Ten Commandments. But these are not just Old Covenant sins. Believers today who live under the New Covenant can be just as guilty of committing them.

Once again, the silence of God is mentioned (v.21). God is long-suffering with sinners, but these wicked people interpreted God's silence as His approval. The people became accustomed to God's patience and mistook it for an inability to do anything about the evil on earth. Their thinking was so confused that they ended up creating gods in their own image.

They had forgotten God and didn't want Him to interfere with their lifestyle. They had a false confidence that they could sin and get away with it.

The honest worshipper (v.22-23)

The books of poetry contrast right and wrong, and sometimes in the same verse. In the case of Psalm 50:22-23, which are the final two verses, this contrast is clearly observed. Asaph listed the characteristics of the kind of worshipper God is seeking.

The true worshipper has a proper fear of the Lord and seeks only to honor Him in his worship. He obeys God's will and experiences the salvation of the Lord. He does not forget God. When you combine these characteristics with verses 14-15–gratitude to God, obedience to His Word, prayer, fear of God, and a desire to glorify God—you have a description of true worshippers who bring joy to the heart of God.

The grace of God is manifested in His patience. Though His people have had and will continue to have problems—sometimes very serious problems—He is still patient with them. Thank God for His mercies which are new every morning.

The Word of God invited his people to repent and to devote themselves once more to a life of godliness, and those who do, will see the salvation of God! Just as there is true worship, there is also false worship. The decision is yours to make—what will you offer to God?

"Just as there is true worship, there is also false worship. The decision is yours to make—what will you offer to God?"

Conclusion

Psalm 50 is concerned with genuine loyalty to God. Loyalty is antithetical to formalism and hypocrisy, as the Lord requires a heart of gratitude. Scripture makes plain that God seeks worshippers who give Him authentic praise from a pure and contrite heart.

And not just any worship will do. Specifically, God seeks those who will worship him in spirit and truth

(John 4:24)–inwardly with the proper heart attitude, yielding humbly to the truth of Scripture.

Worship is to be a lifestyle, a way of living, an ongoing pattern of absolute surrender to God (Romans 12:1). God detests fleshly worship, but He delights in true worship from holy and humble hearts (Philippians 3:3).

May true worshippers offer praise that glorifies God. He alone is worthy. So instead of offering worthless worship such as those described in Psalm 50, let us *"worship the Father in spirit and in truth: for the Father seeketh such to worship him"* (John 4:23).

> *"Worship is to be a lifestyle, a way of living, an ongoing pattern of absolute surrender to God."*

A Kingdom Alignment
Psalm 51

Chapter 11

During his lifetime, King David did what had pleased the Lord all the days of his life, except *"in the matter of Uriah the Hittite"* (1 Kings 15:5). Psalm 51 is David's prayer of confession after Nathan the prophet confronted him with his sin against Uriah (2 Samuel 32:11-12).

The superscription relates the context of the psalm to David's heinous sin with Bathsheba (2 Samuel 11:1-12:25) and the prophet Nathans's subsequent rebuke of David for the adulterous act.

The lament form of the psalm suitably fits the spirit of contrition and prayer for restoration. Gone are the questions; what remains is a soul deeply aware of sin, of having offended God, and of its desperate need of God's grace.

Psalm 51 opens with David's confession of sin, for which he asks God's forgiveness. He requests divine instruction, presents to the Lord a broken spirit as a sacrifice, and then commits himself to the instruction of sinners.

Confession of our sins to God is essential. It is saying the same thing about sin that God does. It is agreeing with God about our sin and its negative impact. True confession also involves turning away from, and forsaking, sin.

Cleanse me (v.1-7)

What dirt is to the body, sin is to the inner person, so it was right for David to feel defiled because of what he had done. By committing adultery and murder, he had crossed over the line God had drawn in His Law (transgression). He had missed the mark God had set for him (sin) and had yielded to his twisted sinful nature (iniquity). He had willfully rebelled against God, and no atonement was provided in the Law for such deliberate sins.

David could appeal only to God's mercy, grace, and love. *"Blot out"* refers to a debt that must be paid, and *"cleanse"* refers to a defilement caused by touching something unclean or from disease. "*Wash*" refers to the cleansing of dirty clothing. In Jewish society of that day, to wash and change clothes marked a new beginning in life, and David needed such a new start.

David had certainly sinned against Bathsheba and Uriah, but his greatest responsibility was to the Lord, who had given the Law to His people. Godly Jews saw all sins primarily as offenses against the Lord.

David knew the truth of God's Word and loved it, but he had deliberately lied to himself and to the people and even tried to lie to God. For nearly a year, he attempted to cover up his sins. But God does not allow His children to sin successfully.

"*Hyssop*" was a shrub with hairy stems that could be dipped into liquid, and the priests used hyssop to sprinkle blood or water on people needing ceremonial cleansing.

In desperate need of divine forgiveness, sinners can do nothing but cast themselves on God's mercy. When sin disrupts a sinner's fellowship with the Lord, he or she has no right to divine blessings. But the Lord has promised to forgive, and his forgiveness is based solely on his love and compassion. Therefore, the psalmist appeals to the Lord's love and great compassion. Forgiveness is an act of divine grace whereby sin is blotted out, and sinners are cleansed by the washing away of their sins.

> *"In desperate need of forgiveness, sinners can do nothing but cast themselves on God's mercy."*

Restore me (v.8-12)

David's sins had affected his whole person: his eyes, mind, ears and bones, heart and spirit, hands, and lips. Such is the high cost of committing sin. He even used the metaphor of broken bones to indicate the internal pain he felt because of the sin he had committed.

Broken bones have a way of naturally healing, for God designed them to do so. Therefore, to suggest God broke his bones was David's way of saying he was broken and vulnerable before God. David knew if God could break him, God could also heal him.

David needed a total transformation. He opened himself to full inspection and expected God to cleanse him from all iniquities.

Use me (v.13-19)

David knew if God forgave and restored him, then he would be able to teach others. They, in turn, would experience their own conversion. He knew he would have a testimony if God forgave him.

Being a psalmist and songwriter, David also knew that if God forgave him, his songs would be resplendent of God's righteousness.

As seen from Psalm 50, David realized God was not interested in sacrifices and burnt offerings, but rather, true repentance from the heart. And David knew that the only way God would be pleased was if his heart was rightly restored.

> *"David needed a total transformation. He opened himself to a full inspection, and expected God to cleanse him from all iniquities."*

Conclusion

The first time the phrase *"Holy Spirit"* is used is found in Psalm 51. Understanding that David was a prophet (Acts 2:29-30) and realizing that David wrote both extensively and prophetically of both the first and second coming of Jesus Christ, I conclude then that David knew more about the New Birth message than many in Christianity today.

In Psalm 51, David mentions repentance, washing (baptism), the Holy Spirit, and most importantly, discipleship, and all of these are focused on the vital importance of relationship.

And David wrote all of this before Jesus Christ was born in Bethlehem, before John proclaimed Jesus to be the Lamb of God who takes away the sin of the world, and before Jesus died on the cross and arose from a borrowed tomb on the third day.

David's motive for repentance was a restored relationship with God. This is exactly why Jesus Christ came, *"To wit, that God was in Christ, reconciling the world unto himself, not imputing their trespasses unto them; and hath committed unto us the word of reconciliation"* (2 Corinthians 5:19).

Planted in God's House
Psalm 52

Chapter 12

A psalm of exhortation, this psalm was written, *"when Doeg the Edomite came and told Saul, and said unto him, David is come to the house of Ahimelech."* Filled with jealousy, Saul was so angered by the report that he ordered the entire community massacred by Doeg. Doeg would brutally murder Ahimelech and eighty-four other priests, as well as women, children, infants, and animals. This tragic account of senseless murder is recorded in 1 Samuel 22.

As David took refuge in God, his high tower of safety, he awaited the destruction of his enemy by the Lord. Psalm 52 is a song of bold, confident trust in God, despite the threats of Doeg and Saul.

David's foe (v.1-14)

David began with a question of accusation, *"Why boastest thou thyself in mischief, O mighty man?"* Doeg, David's foe, was mighty in doing evil and bragged about his consistent rebellion against truth and righteousness. But he was a disgrace in the eyes of God, an embarrassment to heaven, and a violation of everything God desired. David contrasts Doeg's boasting by retorting, *"the goodness of God endureth continually."* Doeg's evil was temporal, but God's goodness is eternal.

Doeg conspired and organized harm to destroy others. Full of perversity, Doeg's mouth was like a sharpened razor, cutting, penetrating, and killing. What he said brought the bloody destruction of others. His words were consistent with deceitful practices, and he refused to control his tongue.

If someone gossips to you, rest assured they will gossip about you. So, beware who and what you listen to. Beware also of the fruit of bitterness; it defiles you and many others.

> *"Doeg's evil was temporal, but God's goodness is eternal."*

The reality of the problem was Doeg's wicked heart. Doeg's sense of morality was wrong. His affections were corrupt and twisted by his depravity. He loved what he should have hated and hated what he should have loved. Thus, his words were deceitful.

Doeg was mighty in his own eyes but insignificant in God's eyes. David was insignificant in the eyes of others, but important to God. David depended on the mercy of the Lord, while Doeg depended on himself and his own resources.

With tongues like sharpened razors, Doeg issued orders and told lies without considering the consequences. Even when he told the truth, he did it with evil intent because he was possessed with an evil spirit.

David's fury (v.5-7)

David pronounced the ultimate destruction of God upon his arrogant enemy. He declared, *"God shall likewise destroy thee for ever."* This would be a just punishment for his ruthless dealings. So devastating would his destruction be that the righteous would see it and be motivated to fear God. And the godly would laugh in derision at the absurdity that anyone would oppose God's will.

Verse 5 is the central verse of the psalm and marks the turning point in David's experience as he contemplated the wickedness of the human heart. He was confident that God would one day judge Saul, Doeg, and all who follow their evil and prideful philosophy of life.

Take notice of the dreadful phrases, *"destroy thee forever... pluck thee out... root thee out..."* God would ultimately punish Doeg for what he did to the priestly community at Nob. This is the ultimate high cost of low living, and it points to the coming Day of the Lord when, once and for all, God's wrath is poured out on the wicked.

You don't have to be on the wrong side of God's judgment. You can either be like David or Doeg; and God in His beautiful mercy allows you to choose. Please consider your choices from the viewpoint of eternity; you only live forever.

> *"You don't have to be on the wrong side of God's judgment."*

David's faith (v.8-9)

In contrast to Doeg, David's faith was in God. He flourished *"like a green olive tree in the house of God."* David was productive, prolific, and prosperous in God's house.

And yet, olives are crushed and pressed, which is how the oil is extracted. Therefore, your trial gives birth to your testimony.

Expressing his reliance upon God's grace, David vowed that he would praise God forever for his many exploits and would hope in God's name. God's name represents the total of all His holy attributes.

The contrast is clear: the wicked are like uprooted trees, but the godly are like flourishing olive trees that are fruitful and beautiful. Saul and Doeg would perish, rejected by the Lord, but David and his dynasty would be safe in the house of the Lord for hundreds of years, until the exile.

It's possible that the tabernacle at Nob had olive trees growing around it, and David would have seen them. Olive trees live for many years and keep bearing fruit (Psalm 1:1-3; 92:12-15; Jeremiah 17:7-8).

"Your trial gives birth to your testimony."

Conclusion

Doeg was a plant in God's house spying for Saul. David was planted in God's house like a green olive tree. Which would you rather be? The choice is up to you. Choose wisely, as eternity is a long time. Do you want to be a plant, spying on whom you can devour with gossip? Or do you want to be planted and established in God, bringing forth fruit that pleases Him?

The battle between the flesh and the Spirit will continue until Jesus Christ returns. There has always been a certain amount of evil in high places, and God's people must learn to handle it in a godly manner. Therefore, let us heed David's words, *"I will wait on thy name."* This means David hoped and depended on the character of God to vindicate him.

Though evil men seem to triumph, we must continue to obey and serve the Lord and not get discouraged. God will have the last laugh, and He cannot be bribed or bought. Wait on His name, *"for it is good before thy saints."*

> *"Doeg was a plant in God's house, spying for Saul. David was planted in God's house like a green olive tree. Which would you rather be?"*

The Fallacy of Atheism!
Psalm 53

Chapter 13

The word *"fool"* is God's appraisal of anyone who tries to live without Him. It is nothing short of spiritual insanity to attempt to live apart from God. And yet, so many people around the world live without God and depend on themselves for all their needs. God says this person is a fool.

This was David's appraisal of the entire human race apart from the grace of God in Psalm 53. Unbelief makes a person a fool—not a person who is mentally deficient, but rather, one who is morally depraved and spiritually destitute.

An amazing similarity exists between Psalm 14 and Psalm 53, and yet there are differences. Where Psalm 14 is personal, Psalm 53 is private. Whereas Psalm 14 is pragmatic, Psalm 53 is prophetic. Whereas Psalm 14 is about the past, Psalm 53 is about the future.

Psalm 53 is a wisdom psalm in which David lamented the total depravity and moral foolishness of humanity. No matter how cleverly man may try to arrange his life, he is still inherently evil and incapable of being good on his own. Jesus said, *"there is none good but one, that is, God"* (Mark 10:18).

There is only one known cure for the deadly plague of sin, and that is the Lord Jesus Christ. He alone can remove the heart of stone and replace it with a heart of flesh. Man's nature is corrupt, perverse, and sinful (Jeremiah 17:9-10). God is the only One who can transform you from the inside out.

This inborn corruption extends to every part of man. As a result of the fall of Adam and the spread of sin to the entire human race, his mind, his emotions, and his will have been polluted by sin. Consequently, *"there is none that doeth good."* Therefore, Jesus Christ came to make us good again (2 Corinthians 5:21).

> *"God is the only One who can transform you from the inside out."*

The fool described (v.1)

The fool does not mean a person of mental incompetence, but a person of moral insensitivity and spiritual ignorance. He rejects and ignores God saying, *"There is no God."* At the very center of his being, in the depth of his soul, he rejects the idea of God ruling over him, but not necessarily the existence of God.

He is a practical atheist, not necessarily an intellectual one. He lives as if there is no God with whom he must deal. He orders his life as if there is no heaven, no hell, no final judgment, no eternal punishment. He may believe God exists, but he does not believe God will judge him for his sinful life.

The result of this blatant rejection of God is a corrupt life. The refusal of God always leads to the corruption of a person's life; the two are inseparably bound together. Lumping together all unbelievers, David declared that they all are corrupt in their inner person or essential being. Their ways are full of injustice and iniquity. All their dealings are an abhorrence to the One True God because they are so unjust, lacking a sense of what is right. Because their personal character is corrupt, their practical conduct is inevitably the same.

Consequently, David's summation is, *"there is none that doeth good."* No one apart from God's grace can practice what is pleasing to the Lord. All their deeds are displeasing to God; in fact, even their best efforts to perform good works is all in vain. The grand total of all of man's righteousness equals filthy rags (Isaiah 64:6).

> *"Because their personal character is corrupt, their practical conduct is inevitably the same."*

The fool discovered (v.2-4)

God looks from heaven to see if anyone understands and seeks Him. He ponders if anyone grasps the seriousness of their sinful rebellion. God wonders if anyone has considered the ramifications of the fallacy of their atheism?

And this is not the first time God looked down. Just three chapters after Adam's sin, the world has become so full of depravity that God repents for making man on the earth. Yet, while God was looking down, Noah was looking up and found grace in God's eyes.

Most sinners do not understand what awaits them as they continue in their evil ways. Without the Holy Spirit, all people are running away from God. And rather than seeking God, the opposite occurs;

everyone turns away from God and goes his own way.

These evildoers are those *"who eat up my people as they eat bread."* They bring great persecution and opposition to true believers. With a voracious appetite for harm, they devour and consume God's people as men eat bread. Therefore, it is not surprising that from this state of spiritual deadness, *"they have not called upon God."*

The world is filled with such people who defend and fund the murder of unborn children, who declare the Bible to be hate speech, who are practical atheists–they believe that God exists, but they do not believe He will judge them. Thus, they devour God's people like they devour bread. Is there hope for such people? Yes, if they repent and are born again (John 3:3-8; Acts 2:38-39). But if the fool does not repent, destruction awaits him.

> *"Most sinners do not understand what awaits them as they continue in their evil ways."*

The fool destroyed (v.5)

David anticipated the judgment of the wicked, a devastation so certain that the verbs are recorded in the past tense as if it has already occurred. They will be terrified with great fear because God will unleash his fiery judgment and wrath upon them. Those who do not fear God, will be filled with great dread, because He will come in destructive power to rout his enemies.

Regarding this outpouring of divine wrath, the scene pictures a battlefield in which God defeated his enemies soundly, leaving them to rot and decay. No disgrace was considered greater for a foreign power, than to have the bones of their defeated army scattered across the battlefield, rather than buried.

God's devastating judgment of the wicked will be so overwhelming. Just read any apocalyptic prophecy from God's Word, and you'll understand what David is describing.

Is there hope? Can there be healing? Can the wicked find their way to God? Is grace available to whomsoever will? Can the practical atheist be saved?

Conclusion, the faithful delivered (v.6)

David prayed for salvation to come, to bring an end to the captivity of his people. Since it would be a few hundred years before the Assyrian and

Babylonian captivity of Israel and Judah, I believe David wrote prophetically of the captivity of sin and the salvation that would come—God manifest in the flesh—to save His people from their sins.

David concluded Psalm 53 on a positive note by asking God to bring salvation. Just as this psalm ends with the possibility of hope, so also the fallacy of atheism can end with a future of atonement. There is still time to share the gospel. There is still hope that someone can be saved from sin. The truth can still be preached, and lives can be transformed by the hope and healing promised through Jesus Christ.

> *"The fallacy of atheism can end with a future of atonement."*

Behold! God is my Helper!
Psalm 54

Chapter 14

Life's trials strip away any vestiges of self-confidence and anchors the soul to a deeper confidence in God. In such a humbling dependence, the born-again believer calls on the name of Jesus Christ and finds strength during his weaknesses. For the Scripture teaches us, *"when I am weak, then am I strong"* (2 Corinthians 12:10). It's not my strength that gets me through; rather, *"I can do all things through Christ which strengtheneth me"* (Philippians 4:13).

Over and again in life, this is precisely where David found himself, calling on the Lord for help in a crisis too big for him to solve on his own. Psalm 54 is the record of his intentional reliance upon God in which he prayed for divine deliverance when he was pursued by Saul. David had rescued an Israelite border town from the Philistines but was still considered a traitor to Saul (1 Samuel 23, 26).

The inscription reveals a clan, the Ziphims, which were from David's own tribe, the tribe of Judah. Although he was hotly pursued by ungodly men who sought to take his life, and betrayed by those in his own tribe, David trusted in the Lord to deliver him. This psalm is a confession of confidence in God that He would protect David from his enemies.

The trial (v.1-3)

David desires God to save and judge him. David knows God is the only source that can truly save him. While David fought many battles in his life, he realizes this one is a spiritual battle that only God can deliver him from.

David knows who has betrayed him, the Ziphims and Saul, yet he calls them strangers (v.3). The use of this word indicates these were ruthless men who had no regard for God. They had become estranged from God and those that were in covenant relationship with God.

Because these individuals rejected God, they became the enemies of God. Therefore, David let God fight this battle for him. He ultimately knew they had betrayed God, not him.

Total trust (v.4-5)

Yet rather than worry about the wicked, David transitions to confident trust stating emphatically, *"God is mine helper!"* This bold statement describes the Lord as the One who sustains, and upholds the soul, of those who trust in Him.

Verse 5 reveals that the resolution of the prayer lies in the conviction that God is just. He will not permit His children to suffer without vindication. Evil will be paid its just reward, and the righteous will be saved. God will have the final say!

The faithlessness of Saul and the Ziphims stands in stark contrast to God's faithfulness. They are enemies who defame Him, yet the Lord is faithful in His relationship to His people. Therefore, David is calm, trusting that God will protect him from his adversity. David is in trouble but knows God is with him.

While I'm certain you have been betrayed by family and friends, it is doubtful you are running for your very life from a wicked king who wants to kill you. So, for you, this psalm is applicable as you deal with the difficult news from the doctor. Or maybe you are going through a divorce. You may be dealing with the loss of your job and wonder if you'll be able to pay your bills this month. Regardless of what you're facing today, and regardless of what any doctor, lawyer, banker, officer, or anyone has said, I encourage you to shout, "Behold! God is MY Helper!"

Total triumph (v.6-7)

Anticipating the certainty of divine help, David burst forth in spontaneous praise and worship before his miracle happened. He did not allow his bleak circumstances to change his knowledge of God. He remained convinced that God was good, even amid his adversity. Such is the focus of strong faith.

David has the assurance that God heard his prayers, even before God rescued him. He acknowledged that he had been delivered from all his troubles in the past. Surely God would do so again in the present. God is in trouble and delivers the righteous out of all trouble.

All trouble.

All!

The resolution of the psalm shines forth in a victory hymn of thanksgiving. Beyond the present tragedy is a future that may be shared with others in the company of God.

> *"God is in trouble and delivers the righteous out of all trouble."*

Conclusion

In every painful ordeal, God is a help to His people. He is the all-sufficient One who sustains them through deep waters. God is the Deliverer of His people who, according to His perfect timing, rescues the righteous from harm.

God is good all the time and is to be trusted in every stormy trial. Even when attacked by others, believers should praise God who rescues His people from trouble.

One of the secrets to trusting God is to remember His faithfulness in past times. Like David in this psalm, we should remember that the many triumphs God has given us over our foes in the past, are proof that we can and should trust Him in the present.

Jesus dismissed crowds but invited disciples to go through storms. Can God trust you with a storm? And whether He calms the storm or the sailor, can you trust that He is your Helper?

Learn the lesson of Psalm 54. David didn't blame God for the problem because he knew the problem was from his enemy. It's like the following story:

A boy's toy boat went out of reach on a pond one day and started floating away. A man on the other side started throwing rocks at the boat, and the boy became horrified at what might happen. But then he realized that the rocks were going over his toy boat and making ripples that finally pushed the boat back to shore and into the boy's hands.

It may appear God is throwing rocks at us, or even allowing the enemy to throw them at us. But remember, those rocks are creating ripples, which will bring back what seems to be lost!

If the situation looks bleak right now and if your heart is overwhelmed today, go to the Rock that is higher than your situation. God has always been there for you, He's presently helping you, and He will always be there for you. I again encourage you to say it out loud, *"Behold, God is mine helper!"*

"Can God trust you with a storm?"

But I Will Trust in You
Psalm 55

Chapter 15

It's likely that this psalm was written early in Absalom's rebellion (2 Samuel 15-17) when David was still in Jerusalem and the revolt was gathering momentum. If so, then the "friend" of verses 12-14 and 20-21 had to be David's counselor Ahithophel who sides with Absalom.

Many commentators claim that the king and his officers did not know about Ahithophel's treachery until after David had fled the city, but this is not clearly stated in Scripture. David was a man with keep discernment, and it is difficult to believe that his closest advisor's treachery was hidden from him.

If this psalm was David's prayer while still in Jerusalem, then his prayer in 2 Samuel 15:31 is simply a repetition of verse 9.

David, surrounded by expressions of animosity, not only from old foes but now even from those he believed to be his friends, pours out his heart before the Lord. The mood of the psalm moves from despair to complaint, to a note of confidence in the Lord. There is also a comparison of David's betrayal, to that of Judas and his betrayal of Jesus Christ.

We can look within at our feelings (v.1-5)

In verse 1, David opened with a plea to the Lord that He would not hide His face from his supplications. David knew that his own negligence as a father, had turned Absalom against his father, the Lord, and the nation. He also knew that the revolt was part of the discipline that Nathan the prophet promised, because of David's adultery, and the murder of Uriah.

What David heard and saw in the city distressed him greatly, and he realized that his own life was in danger. The opposition was bringing trouble upon him the way soldiers fling stones at the enemy or roll down rocks upon them.

But David's concern was for the safety of his people, and the future of the Lord's promises to his own dynasty. He felt like everything was falling apart, and there was no hope. It's natural to look at our feelings and express our fears, but that is not the way to solve the problems.

David turns unto the Lord and asks him to listen. He does not pretend that there is no problem. His prayer flows out of deep despair. David is continually troubled and cannot find rest within himself. He is full of inner turmoil.

David yearns to escape his situation. He is full of anguish, fear, and horror. He is paralyzed emotionally and physically as he mulls over the present evil. He is weak and helpless. His heart is palpitating like the heart of a woman in labor, and fear overtakes him.

This is the result of only looking within at our feelings. Our hearts become overwhelmed, our minds play tricks on us, and if we let fear run its course, then we will lose our faith and hope.

It's ok to be honest about your feelings, but remember, *"the heart is deceitful above all things, and desperately wicked"* (Jeremiah 17:9). If your heart is overwhelmed, go to the Rock (Psalm 61:2), and realize God is greater than your heart (1 John 3:20).

> *"If we let fear run its course, then we will lose our faith and hope."*

We can look beyond for a safe refuge (v.6-8)

When we find ourselves in the middle of trouble, our first thought is, "How can I get out of this?" But the dedicated disciple asks, "What can I get out of this?"

David had learned some strategic lessons while hiding in the wilderness from Saul. But in his later years, he had some more important lessons to learn. The human heart longs for a safe and peaceful refuge, far from the problems and burdens of life.

Elijah fled from the place of ministry and hid in a cave. Jeremiah longed for a quiet lodge where he might get away from the wicked people around him. Yet, when given the opportunity to leave Judah, like a true shepherd, he remained with the people.

Doves can fly long distances and they seek safe refuges in the high rocks. But we don't need wings like a dove so we can fly away from the storm. We need wings like an eagle so we can fly above the storm.

Another manner of expressing David's deep despair, is in the imagery of escape. How he wishes to find the quiet serenity of the desert, far away from civilization! How he wishes to find protective shelter from a sudden storm. But is that the correct answer? Crowds get dismissed, but disciples are privileged to go through storms.

This desire to want to look beyond and be hidden away is isolation. While we all need times of aloneness with God, apart from others, no man is an island! God did not intend for you to be alone and isolated. It is ok to look beyond your problem and trust in God; it is not ok to look beyond to escape from your problem.

You need the Church, and the Church needs you. *"Two are better than one...and a threefold cord is not quickly broken"* (Ecclesiastes 4:9, 12).

> *"God did not intend for you to be alone and isolated."*

We can look around at the circumstances (v.9-15, 20-21)

David wasn't living in denial, he knew what was going on around him, and he directed operations in a masterful manner. But he also prayed that God would bring confusion to Absalom's ranks, and that's exactly what happened in verse 9. The Lord used Hushai to influence Absalom, to reject Ahithophel's counsel, and this led to the defeat of Absalom's forces.

Among the rebels, David singled out one person who broke his heart, and that was Ahithophel. As David's counselor, Ahithophel was not equal to the king in rank or authority, but he was very close to David. They had worshiped the Lord together, but now Ahithophel was counseling David's son to rebel against his father. Ahithophel violated the covenant of friendship with David.

If you only look around at the circumstances, you risk fear overtaking you, causing you to trust in your own strength and wisdom. Yes, you need to consider what you're up against, and exercise wise discernment, but don't forget to look up to God for His help.

The enemy wants you to focus on the problem. His purpose is to make you forget your purpose. Do not take the bait of the enemy by focusing on the bleakness of your situation. Remember, God is in trouble with you, so let your faith in God cause you to look up.

> *"If you only look around at the circumstances, you risk fear overtaking you, causing you to trust in your own strength and wisdom."*

We can look up to God and trust Him (v.16-19, 22-23)

While it is both normal for us to hope for a quick way of escape, and important for us to understand our feelings and circumstances, it's far more important to look up to God and ask for His help.

David could no longer lead an army into battles, but he was able to pray that God would defeat the rebel forces. And God did answer those prayers of his. David shows us in this psalm that praying always, during good times or bad times, is the only way to truly handle the storms of life. David's throne was in danger, but God's throne was secure.

During his difficult years of preparation, David had experienced many changes, and this taught him to trust the God who never changes (Malachi 3:6, James 1:17).

Absalom and his friends had lived in luxury and ease and knew very little about the challenge of changing circumstances, so they had no faith in God or fear of God. A prosperous life is an easy life until you find yourself in the middle of the storm, and then you discover how ill prepared you are. For what life does to us depends on what life finds in us.

The beautiful promise of verse 22 is repeated in 1 Peter 5:7 and reveals that whether in good times or bad, in times of pain and sorrow, the Lord is still in control. David was in trouble; therefore, God was in trouble with him.

David was confident that the Lord is just in His acts of deliverance, and that will result in peace, even though the opposition has been great. David's hope was based on the truth that God is enthroned forever.

Your problem cannot dethrone God. Your situation is not too difficult for God to handle. Your boat may be rocked by the winds and waves, but your God walks on waves, commands the winds, and they obey Him! God is in trouble with you!

> *"David's throne was in danger, but God's throne was secure."*

Conclusion

Psalm 55 is a wisdom psalm, teaching that God is not mocked. Whatever a person sows, that will he also reap. If he sows to the flesh, he will reap corruption. If he sows seeds of deceit, treachery, and betrayal, he will reap a bitter harvest of destruction and death. As such, Ahithophel committed suicide, and Absalom was killed in a cruel manner.

Because God is holy and just, His saints who are often betrayed and afflicted will find a sure defense in the Lord. Rather than seek their own revenge, born-again believers need only to trust in God.

Explaining the events surrounding His second coming, Jesus said, *"And when these things begin to come to pass, then look up, and lift up your heads; for your redemption draweth nigh"* (Luke 21:28). But you do not have to wait until His coming to look up. If you are in trouble, go ahead and look up, for God is with you.

Refuse to look within, as this can lead to your feelings overriding your faith and producing fear. Refuse to look beyond, as this can lead to a desire to escape from reality. Refuse to look at your circumstance through the lens of your flesh, for this can lead to trusting in your own strength. Instead, choose to look up and trust God with all your heart, soul, mind, and strength.

> *"If you are in trouble, go ahead and look up, for God is with you."*

This I Know That God is For Me!
Psalm 56

Chapter 16

The historical setting of Psalm 56 is found in 1 Samuel 21. David is on the run from Saul, and his life is in danger. He had fled so quickly that he does not take a weapon with him. He flees to Ahimelech, the priest of Nob. He eats bread reserved for the priests, and then he asks him for a sword. Ahimelech then gives him Goliath's sword, which was behind the ephod. Thinking this is what he needs, David declares, *"There is none like that; give it me"* (1 Samuel 21:9).

Yet, after leaving Ahimelech, David is still afraid and very much fearful. In fact, he flees to his archenemies, the Philistines, and acts like a madman, frothing at the mouth, to disguise himself. For good reason: he's in Gath, the hometown of Goliath, whom he killed a few years earlier.

Still fearful for his life, David flees to the cave of Adullam, where he is joined by an army; however, not an army like you'd think. These men are *"distressed... in debt... and discontented..."*

David ensures the safety of his family, fearing that Saul would try to capture them to either kill, or at the very least use them as leverage against him. And if you haven't caught it yet, David was afraid.

Sometimes we are in the same dilemma as David; we are running scared and don't know what will happen. But is that the answer? Remember, *"God hath not given us the spirit of fear; but of power, and of love, and of a sound mind"* (2 Timothy 1:7).

Why do we fear the economy when God is our provider? Why do we fear the doctor's report when God is our healer? Why do we fear man when God is greater than all?

Yet, like David, we fear, run, and hide. But that's not how or where the story ends. Stay tuned for a divine shift.

In the Scripture, you can read how a prophet, a man of God by the name of Gad, went to David with a word from God: *"Abide not in the hold; depart, and get thee into the land of Judah. Then David departed, and came into the forest of Hareth"* (1 Samuel 22:5). Yet, as soon as David obeys the command, he is discovered by friends of Saul, and Saul thinks he has him cornered.

Have you ever obeyed the Word of the Lord, only for things to go worse? Then you're not alone. David, and a host of other Bible characters, experienced things getting worse before they got better. But, somewhere between that word from the Lord through the prophet Gad, and the next chapter in 1 Samuel, David has a change of heart.

He's no longer running in fear; he's obeying the Word of the Lord despite negative circumstances. And there's something else. Instead of reaching for a weapon, he's asking for an ephod from Abiathar, the priest. This happens at Keilah (1 Samuel 23:9) and again at Ziklag (1 Samuel 30:7).

You see, the first time David went to the priest of Nob and grabbed the sword of Goliath, it was behind the ephod. Sometime after the word from the prophet of God, David has learned he didn't need the sword; he needed the ephod.

And for all those wondering how this ties back to Psalm 56, thanks for bearing with me. Psalm 56 was written as David's testimony of how he went from fearing man, to trusting God.

Something happened in the life of David that caused him to alter his course, and that something was a word from God. When you have a Word from God, you have all you need!

No wonder David said twice, *"In God I will praise his word"* (Psalm 56:4, 10). That one word from God, which David obeyed immediately, caused a divine shift in his life. He was afraid before the prophet Gad visited him and delivered God's Word. But, after that encounter, David said, *"I will not fear what flesh can do unto me"* (v.4) and *"I will not be afraid of what man can do unto me"* (v.11).

> *"When you have a Word from God, you have all you need!*

I do not believe this psalm was written after the complete victory. I believe David wrote Psalm 56 after he received a word from God. I believe after Gad delivered the Word from God, David had a prayer meeting, and remembered the valley of Elah and a certain uncircumcised Philistine. David began remembering that it was God who brought the victory in that valley.

Conclusion

The next time you're overwhelmed by fear, remember what David learned: *"This I know: God is on my side!"* (Psalm 56:9, New Living Translation).

Open your Bible and let God speak to you. Underline, highlight, or memorize God's Word, and when the devil starts lying to you, remind him he belongs under your feet (Luke 10:19).

The Bible is meant to be experienced. It is inerrant and infallible because God cannot lie (Titus 1:2). And while you should study the historical context of each passage, drawing out all the rich truth therein, you should also realize there is a personal application meant for you.

Such is the case with Psalm 56. David was in trouble, but God sent His prophet, Gad, to remind David that he was not alone. Maybe this chapter was meant for you, to remind you that you are not alone, and that God is with you.

> *"When the devil starts lying to you, remind him he belongs under your feet."*

Be Exalted, O God
Psalm 57

Chapter 17

Psalm 57 picks up where Psalm 56 ended. And according to the introduction of the psalm, David is still in a cave. This is the reason that I explained in the last chapter that David did not write Psalm 56 (or 57) after the victory. He wrote both before the victory, believing God would perform His Word.

Testimony at any time is great, but there's something special about declaring your victory before it happens. There's something about giving God praise and worship before the miracle manifests. Praise is great all the time, but when you praise God during the problem, and thank Him during the trial, it produces a most precious aroma of worship to God.

Psalms 56 and 57 portray confidence in the Lord during adversity. Both psalms reflect similar situations, and when read together, along with the account recorded in 1 Samuel chapters 21-23, a clearer picture of what David experienced unfolds.

> *"Testimony at any time is great, but there's something special about declaring your victory before it happens."*

Praise on purpose fulfills God's purpose (v.1-3)

When you praise on purpose, you fulfill God's purpose! David depended upon God to see him through his trials. His worship and prayer turned the cave he was hiding in, into the Holy of Holies, where he could hide under God's wings. David was in trouble, but God was in trouble with him.

The Ark of the Covenant was covered with the Mercy Seat, which had two cherubs, whose wings touched each other, and their faces bowed toward the middle. David had seen the Ark and knew its significance. The cave he was in, soon became a prayer room, a holy room, and a place where God's presence manifested to him.

When you praise on purpose, regardless of your situation, regardless of your location, God will show up because God *"inhabitest the praises of Israel"* (Psalm 22:3). And since born-again believers are the Israel of God (Galatians 6:16), this means that God makes you His temple, placing His throne in your life, dwelling within your praise!

In Psalm 55, David wished for the wings of a dove to fly away from his problem. That is the wrong way of dealing with problems. But after a word from God in Psalm 56, notice David no longer wishes for wings of a dove to fly away, but rather to be hidden under the wings of God in prayer and praise. David was in the secret place of the Almighty in that cave.

Part of God's purpose was deliverance from Saul and David's other enemies; but a greater part of God's purpose was for David to learn some valuable lessons about trusting God no matter what.

It's easy to trust God when there is plenty of money in the bank account. It's easy to trust God when the doctor's report gives you a clean bill of health. It's easy to trust God when there are no problems to face. But trusting Him in a cave, not knowing if you should sleep because of a fear of death, teaches you to trust in God no matter what.

Although David's enemies not only appear to be more equipped, but also indeed outnumber him, he learns in that cave that God is *"Most High"* and that God will shame his enemies. David began to remember that God is the superlative majority and can do the miraculous against impossible odds.

When you turn your troubling circumstance into the Holy of Holies, and pray and praise on purpose, you can be assured that God will show up and fulfill His purpose in you, through you, and for you. Jesus Christ is the same yesterday, today, and forever!

> *"God is the superlative majority, and can do the miraculous against impossible odds."*

Praise through problems (v.4-6)

David expresses that he feels like his soul is in a lion's den (v.4) and that he is in a deadly pit (v.6), but in the middle of these two verses, David boldly proclaims, *"Be thou exalted, O God, above the heavens; let thy glory be above all the earth."*

As you're reading this sentence, pause for a minute and recognize what's in your peripheral vision without taking your eyes off this book.

Now, imagine that this book is your destiny, your God-given purpose, and whatever is in your peripheral vision are the distractions of life, like David's feelings in Psalm 57:4 and 6.

If you keep your eyes on this book (your destiny), you will finish it. But, if you focus on whatever is in your peripheral vision, you will become distracted from finishing this book.

This type of mental discipline is what David exercised in Psalm 57:4-6. He not only let us know what was in his peripheral vision, but he also highlighted the One upon whom he was fully focused, namely God, who is exalted above the heavens and the earth. David did not gloss over or deny his feelings. He did not pretend that they did not exist. Instead, amid all the trouble surrounding him, he chose to focus on God!

Will you choose to focus on God, regardless of the trouble you're in?

Praise among the peoples (v.7-11)

Once you've praised and prayed with purpose, and praised and prayed through your problems, it's easy to praise God among the peoples. But again, I remind you, David is still in the cave and hasn't experienced deliverance, yet!

In many psalms, we see this same call for praise among the peoples and nations. The best way to remember God's Word is to share it with others.

Conclusion

The God who permits believers to fall into fiery trials, is the same God who can deliver them from those troubles. He created the stormy wind which obeys His word, and He calms the same wind by His word. It was God who allowed Satan to attack Job, but it was God who also gave Satan strict parameters and boundaries.

When surrounded by adversity, will you look at the dilemma, or will you look to your Deliverer? When you're in your cave like David, will you turn it into a pity party, or have a prayer and praise party? Will you choose to see God above and beyond every circumstance, sickness, or problem you may be in?

"Will you look at the dilemma, or will you look to your Deliverer?"

Surely There is a God Who Judges the Earth
Psalm 58

Chapter 18

An inseparable connection exists between a person's character and his conduct. The former is the source of the latter. Some people claim that a leader's private life does not matter, that we should only be concerned about his public performance. But what a leader is internally, will always show up externally.

This is the focus of Psalm 58, a lament psalm, filled with righteous anger about corrupt leaders who lord it over the people. This psalm is a passionate prayer of David for God to judge corrupt judges and to make right every wrong suffered at their hands.

Contained in this psalm is David's outcry against human injustice on the earth, and his earnest plea that God would devastate and destroy those ungodly rulers and judges who harmed the righteous. David was confident that God would eventually punish all wrongdoers and reward the righteous.

How do we answer the injustice of abortion and those who fight to retain the right to do so? How do we pray when literally millions of Christians every year are persecuted for their faith, many of them unto death? Where do we find hope when humanity spreads lies and prejudices in society, our schools, and on our streets?

What do we say regarding those who can hire an entire firm of high-priced, high-powered attorneys, and receive little to no punishment for their crime? Our only hope, in a day when persecuted believers find themselves in a polluted world suffering oppression for righteousness' sake, is to know and declare with David, *"verily he is a God that judgeth the earth."*

In such dark hours, believers must call out for God to exalt Himself and demonstrate His sovereignty over ungodly leaders. It may appear that God has turned a blind eye to all the injustice in our world, but it only appears that way. Don't give in to fear.

Saul's ungodly rule

During David's exile years, Saul led the nation down a path of political and spiritual ruin as he disobeyed God's law and opposed God's anointed king.

Saul was surrounded by a group of flatterers who fed his ego and catered to his foolish whims. He put into places of authority people who used their offices for personal gain and not for the good of the nation of Israel. They wanted to get as much as they could before the kingdom collapsed.

David himself had been treated illegally, and it's likely that many of his men had lost all they had, because they followed David. 1 Samuel 22:2 reveals these men were *"in distress...in debt...and...discontented."*

Psalm 58 is an imprecatory psalm, calling for judgment on the enemies of God. Because of this, many ignore and skip over it, feeling it does not apply. And to a certain extent, they have a point. Jesus taught we are to pray for our enemies, not wish for their destruction. But, since all Scripture is profitable, we must realize these imprecatory psalms do point to the day when God will vindicate the righteous, and exact vengeance on the wicked for their unrepentant sin.

Confident of God's vindication of the righteous, David's prophetic understanding is a comfort to God's people, whenever they are harassed or maligned. And as this psalm would have comforted those who heard it sung, so we, too, find comfort in knowing *"he is a God that judgeth the earth."*

Identity crisis

There are three times when David was tempted to take matters into his own hands. In one of those instances, David cut off the cords of Saul's garment; but God rebuked him, and he was convicted by the Spirit of God. Why? Because the cord he had cut off was one of the cords that hung on the bottom of their garments and represented the Word and the Name of God. In other words, David was convicted that he had nearly cut Saul off from God's word and God's name; however, he realized that Almighty God is the only One who has the right to do that.

Have you prayed for your enemies as much as you've posted about them? Can you be Christ-like and forgive your Judas who betrays you? Can you forgive the Simon Peter in your life who denies he knows you when you need him most? Can you forgive those who abandon you in your hour of need? Can you return good for the evil done to you?

"Have you prayed for your enemies as much as you've posted about them?"

A remnant of righteousness

Since the fall of Adam, there have been injustices, prejudices, and sin of every sort. But since the fall of Adam, there's always been a remnant!

Seth called on the name of the Lord.
Noah found grace in the eyes of the Lord.
Abraham faithfully obeyed and believed God.
Joseph forgave his brothers.
Rahab repented and saved her family.
Ruth forsook Moab and followed God.
Esther fasted, prayed, and saved her people.
Daniel did not defile himself.
Hananiah, Mishael, and Azariah did not bow to idols.

Although these, and so many more, were unable to partake of the promise, they endured hardship and injustices while seeking for it, and ultimately died in the faith (Hebrews 11).

Equally, the New Testament continues to reveal the remnant who accepted Jesus Christ as the Messiah, discarding the Rabbinical teachings that the Messiah would be a warrior who would overthrow their oppressors.

Applying Psalm 58 in the present

I weep, and hurt, and even get angry every time I hear of anyone being treated unjustly. In my youth, one of my favorite comics was *The Punisher*, because he would help people receive justice who had otherwise been denied it.

But, as I read Psalm 58, with the understanding of the eternal lake of fire for those who do not repent of their wickedness and sin, I cannot think like a vigilante. Instead, I must pray and say like David, *"he is a God that judgeth the earth."* I must let God be the judge, and I must pray that my enemies repent and find grace in the eyes of the Lord.

Even David, who had three opportunities to kill Saul, wept when he received the news of his death. David did not rejoice, but rather, mourned the loss. And maybe, in part, because he knew Saul died without truly repenting.

Conclusion

When God judges the earth, there will be no appeals and no attorneys to say, "objection your honor." There will be no jury to deliberate or appellate courts to overturn His verdict. God alone will be the Judge. And if you think you are angry over the injustices, imagine how much angrier God is. He is angry with the wicked every day (Psalm 7:11), and has prepared His throne for judgment, and will judge the world in His righteousness (Psalm 9:7-8).

God sees the sin, mistreatment, injustice, and prejudice of the world (Psalm 10:12-14). And when judgment day arrives, everyone will reap what they've sown (Psalm 11:4-7).

In Psalm 58, sin was practiced (v.1-5), sin was punished (v.6-9), and salvation was promised (v.10-11). Nothing much has changed since the writing of Psalm 58, with the exception that Jesus Christ came, died, and rose again, bringing new life. And God is not willing that any should perish, but that all should repent (2 Peter 3:9).

The very Word of God that is living and active, is the same Word of God that will be used to judge the world! It is God's constitution! We will all have to give an account to God. Did we let our circumstances dictate our actions? Did we forgive our enemies? Did we obey God's Word? It's more than just being born again and coming to church twice a week; it's about being the church daily, for, *"verily he is a God that judgeth the earth."*

> *"God is not willing that any should perish, but that all should repent."*

Who Are You?
Psalm 59

Chapter 19

The historical setting for this psalm of David is found in 1 Samuel 19 when Saul plotted and planned to kill David twice. First by himself, and secondly, by sending his guards, who were tricked by Michal as she helped David escape. And although that is the historical setting, and although this psalm is classified as one of the imprecatory psalms which call for God's judgment, the focus of Psalm 59 is not on the enemy, but rather on the God who is able and willing to deliver from the enemy.

I originally preached Psalm 59 on July 7, 2019. Beginning earlier that year in March, God was challenging the church I pastor to identify ourselves the way He identifies us, rather than any other way.

We must not identify with fear, insecurity, circumstance, sin, the past, or even our ethnicity. Instead, like David, we need to identify ourselves with God and how He sees us and who He calls us to be. Instead of having an identity crisis, we identify ourselves in Christ, through Christ, and by Christ.

Your Strength (v.9, 17)

Despite his life being in danger and realizing this would be the last time he would see his best friend, Jonathan; David uses this psalm to focus on God. David refers to God's strength as both his reason to continue, and as his defense.

As seen in most of David's psalms, he takes his concerns and requests to God. He could have strategized and convened his war council, but instead, David chose to pray and seek God's counsel. David chose to focus on God's strength, not his own.

Not only did David bring his problem to God in prayer, but David also chose to trust God with the outcome, stating he would wait on God (v.9). David knew God would rescue him from trouble, and it would be in His perfect timing. David knew God would have the last laugh against those who were hostile and scoffed at him (v.8). Therefore, he waited on and trusted in God.

Relying on God's strength and mercy, David knew God would bring swift defeat to his enemies. David's trouble would soon turn into triumph as God delivered him.

For whatever trouble you are in, let God's Word be your strength today. Be reminded through His Word that you are not alone and that He will never forsake you. Trust God's timing in your trouble; He never fails (Zephaniah 3:5) and He cannot lie (Titus 1:2).

> *"Trust God's timing in your trouble."*

Your Shield

Being a skilled warrior, David would understand the value of a shield in battle. David was also familiar with the metaphor of God being his shield. David would have been familiar with the Word of the LORD to Abram, *"Fear not, Abram: I am thy shield, and thy exceeding great reward."*

David would also have been familiar with Deuteronomy 33:29, which states, *"O people saved by the LORD, the shield of thy help, and who is the sword of thy excellency!"*

And in fact, this is not the first time David himself has referred to God as his or Israel's shield. In 2

Samuel 22:31 and 36, David refers to God as *"a buckler to all them that trust in him"* and as *"the shield of thy salvation."*

In addition to Psalm 59 being an imprecatory psalm, it also includes what scholars call the Divine Warrior metaphor. The words *"defend"* (v.1) and *"defense"* (v.9, 16-17) correlate with *"O Lord our shield"* (v.11), and reveals that God is the Ultimate Warrior, protecting and defending His own.

David is a warrior. He is skilled in battle. He serves with men who are brave and have performed great feats in battle. Yet, David knows this is a battle he must let God fight.

Interestingly, when David referred to God's strength, he said, *"O my strength"* (v.17). But when David refers to God as a shield, he said, *"O Lord our shield"* (v.11). While each of us needs a personal relationship with God, we also need to realize we are not alone. The whole premise of this third volume is to highlight those psalms where individuals realized they were not alone in their trouble. God is with us in our trouble, but so are others. You may feel alone, but you're not. God is our shield, just like He is also our Father (Matthew 6:9).

> *"God is the Ultimate Warrior, protecting and defending His own."*

Your song

David could sing in the middle of this trouble. Read that again. In fact, the superscription explains this was a song for the choir to sing. *"To the chief Musician, Altaschith. Michtam of David; when Saul sent, and they watched the house to kill him."*

It's one thing to sing when everything is going great, the bills are paid, the birds are harmonizing with you, and the temperature is perfect, and life is grand. But David sang when he was surrounded by people waiting to kill him.

The word *"Altaschith"* is a Hebrew word that means, "Set to 'Do Not Destroy.'" Apparently "Do Not Destroy" was some sort of musical arrangement upon which David was writing new lyrics for. Did he mean "Do Not Destroy" as a statement of faith that Saul could not destroy him? Or was it a statement of prayer that God would not destroy Saul? I'll let you decide, but as you decide, consider verse 11, which says, *"Slay them not."*

Because God was David's strength and shield, he had a song to sing despite the enemy and the circumstances. David was able to praise through the pain, and worship in the wilderness. Because of this, David was victorious and not a victim, and God turned his trouble into his testimony.

You may not be in the choir, but you can make a joyful noise. You may not be a psalmist like David, but you can praise and worship God despite your circumstances.

God is your strength and shield. Therefore, you have a reason to sing aloud, praising Him for His mighty acts. You have a right to praise God according to His excellent greatness.

> *"David was able to praise through the pain and worship in the wilderness."*

Conclusion

In the historical setting of Psalm 59, which is found in 1 Samuel 19:11, Michal is called *"David's wife."* Yet, after David became king, Michal mocked him for worshipping when the Ark of the Covenant was returned to Jerusalem. She was then called *"Saul's daughter"* (2 Samuel 6:16). Something had happened in her heart and mind that caused her to be identified with Saul rather than with David.

Saul is clearly the epitome of evil, and David was a man after God's own heart. Who are you identified with? Who are you?

To identify with Christ means you walk in newness of life; the old has passed away, and all things have become new.

On the other hand, to have an identity crisis means you identify with fear, and in so doing, doubt the very God who robed Himself in the flesh to become sin, so you would be able to become His righteousness.

So, who are you? Will you identify with the Creator of life or the accuser of the brethren? Will you identify with the One God and Father of all who is above all, through all, and in you all? Or will you identify with Beelzebub, the lord of the flies?

"To identify with Christ means you walk in newness of life; the old has passed away and all things have become new."

The Transformation From Trouble to Triumph
Psalm 60

Chapter 20

While David was up north fighting the Syrians, the Edomites attacked Israel from the south, doing a great deal of damage. David dispatched Joab with part of the army, and Joab and Abishai defeated Edom in the Valley of Salt, south of the Dead Sea (1 Chronicles 18:12).

David must have written the psalm shortly after hearing the bad news of the invasion by Edom, but the psalm manifests a spirit of trust and confidence that the Lord would give Israel the victory, which He did. The historical context for these battles is recorded in 2 Samuel 8:1-14, 2 Samuel 10:6-18, 1 Chronicles 18:1-13, and 1 Chronicles 19:6-19.

A troubled people (v.1-5)

Verses 1-3 make it evident that adversity had strained the covenantal relationship between God and His people. The people feel rejected and abandoned by God, and long to be reconciled to Him once again.

Rejection, even though for a brief time, is serious because it is a result of God's anger. His anger and its impact are felt throughout. God's people live a meaningless existence without His presence. Israel takes this defeat seriously and soberly because divine abandonment is the most miserable of conditions.

This lament psalm is occasionally interrupted by brief prayers for relief and restoration. The people pray for restoration to the favor of God and for His emotional healing. And so Almighty God raised a banner designating a place where the godly may find refuge under His protection. The godly who fear the Lord will find protection and their confidence in the One true God.

The name of the Lord, and His restored favor, became their battle cry. David, being a man of faith, did not give up, but rallied the people around the Lord's name as their banner!

We must remember when we are faced with such troubling circumstances, we must trust in the Lord our God. If God brought you to the trial, He will also bring you through the trial. God knows what He is doing, and if He allowed difficulty to afflict you, He is also able to deliver you.

Sometimes we do suffer because of mistakes we made, and when we do, let us repent with sincerity and find grace to help in our time of need. Yet, at other times, we suffer because God is wanting to teach us a lesson. And in these times, let us have the courage to ask, "God, what lesson do you want me to learn from this?"

> *"If God brought you to the trial, He will also bring you through the trial."*

A triumphant message (v.6-8)

In verse 6, God answers the prayer of His people, giving an oracle of hope; *"God hath spoken in his holiness."* God reminds His people of His promise that the earth is His, and that no enemy will succeed against Him.

God reminds them He alone is sovereign, not only over Israel, but also over all the nations. God speaks from His holiness, and rejoicing is the immediate result. For when God speaks, what He says comes to pass.

This is a beautifully written account of a prayer request and God's answer to it. It may not be a battlefield such as David and Joab experienced. Maybe your situation is a difficult divorce, or you've been laid off, or maybe a bill is due, and you're not sure how you're going to pay it. Regardless of your trouble, let Psalm 60 encourage you that the same God who is sovereign over every nation, is also sovereign over every situation.

The problem you face has not dethroned God from His sovereignty. The circumstance you're dealing with has not caused God to worry. What you thought was a setback could be God setting you up for a victory. You are about to experience the transformation from trouble to triumph.

"The same God who is sovereign over every nation, is also sovereign over every situation."

A trustworthy Lord (v.9-12)

Verses 9-11 resume God's oracle of hope. David asks the Lord to lead him in victory. He is not looking for a military solution to his problems, such as alliances with other kings, because he knows that their help is worthless. David knows that his help comes from the Lord. The Lord is still with them, and he will bring them through this adversity with renewed strength, joy, and victory.

David earnestly prayed that the Lord would honor His Word and give His beloved people victory over their enemies, and the Lord answered. David did not interpret this setback as the sign of total defeat.

Maybe this defeat was part of God's plan to get the focus off David. After all, the Bible says David was making a name for himself when His focus should have been making a name for God. God had to bring David to a place where his trust was not in himself, or in his capable officers, or in his valiant soldiers, but completely in God alone!

He learned to trust fully in the Lord, and the Lord honored his faith. The enemy would be completely defeated and trampled into the dirt, and Israel would triumph. Israel rallied to the banner of the name of the Lord, and the Lord gave them victory.

"David did not interpret this setback as a sign of total defeat."

Conclusion

There are times when God's people suffer defeat, giving the appearance that God has forsaken them. But such times of difficulty should not drive born-again believers into despair. Rather, this should cause you to experience a deeper dependency on the Lord. This was the experience of David as recorded in Psalm 60. He prayed an urgent prayer for victory after suffering a devastating defeat.

When you face a situation you are struggling with, you should first ask God to reveal to you if this is because of something you did. If so, His grace is sufficient, and you can find a place of repentance. But, if it is not because of something you have done, then ask God what the lesson is that you should learn during this season, and how you can apply it with wisdom for the future.

The timeless lesson of Psalm 60 is clear: only God can give victory in the face of defeat. When you are suffering harm, God can rout your foes and win an overwhelming victory. No matter how great the setback may be, defeat is never final if the grace of God is available.

But, as Psalm 60 illustrates, you must call out to God and ask for the victory. You must make His name great, rather than make a name for yourself. You must use your spiritual weapons of prayer, faith, and God's Word and act with determined resolve.

David's transformation from trouble to triumph, was when God spoke from His holiness. Consider the power of God's Word: it framed the world and holds it together (Colossians 1:17; Hebrews 1:3; 11:3). When Jesus said, "Peace be still," the wind and the waves obeyed His Word (Mark 4:39). Every word of God is proven true (2 Samuel 22:31), so trust God's Word, and when it comes, it will transform your trouble into triumph.

Do you realize that every time you read God's Word, you hear His voice? Read your Bible daily. Listen intently to the preached and taught Word of God. Then, mix God's Word with your faith, and prepare yourself for a holy transformation. Receive God's Word today, spoken from His holiness, and experience the transformation from trouble to triumph.

> *"Only God can give the victory in the face of defeat."*

On Christ, the Solid Rock I Stand
Psalm 61

Chapter 21

The genre of Psalm 61 is an individual lament; any and every born-again believer may claim this prayer as their own. Faith is a living, active confidence in God, a firm reliance upon Him in every circumstance and crisis. This is how David met the trials and troubles thrown against him. He did so with a firm trust in God, and Psalm 61 is the inspired record of another such occasion in his life.

David wrote this prayer at a time when he was removed from Jerusalem and surrounded by trouble.

He was probably fleeing from his rebellious son Absalom, hiding in the protection of the rocky crags, in the higher ground of the Judean wilderness. But David looked beyond the physical rocks to the Lord as his ultimate protection. God was his Rock of refuge!

It's one thing to have faith in the existence of God, but can you trust Him when you do not feel His presence? Can you trust Him even when you don't see the miracle? Can you trust Him while waiting for the answer? When you are in trouble, and you feel all alone, can you trust that God is in trouble with you, even if you cannot see Him? When you feel as if your faith is tested to its limits, you need to trust God despite the trouble you're in (Proverbs 3:5-6).

"Can you trust God when you do not feel His presence?"

Prelude of prayer (v.1-3)

In the first three verses of this psalm, David gives us a prelude to his prayer, in which he reminds God of all He has done and who He is. In a manner well known in the lament psalms, the psalmist calls on the Lord to answer him. Confidence in Christ is not the same thing as arrogance. God wants us to boldly approach His throne of grace!

The nature of the misery is not spelled out, but its effect on the sufferer is. It wears him out so that he becomes weary of life to the point of despair. David seems far from God. He was geographically away from Jerusalem and its representation as the city of the Great King, but he also felt metaphorically distant from God. Yet, David knew God reigned from His exalted throne, high above every situation, and had the ability to deliver every time.

In the present affliction, David recalls the past ways in which the Lord has come through. He has found God to be a refuge from trouble and a strong tower. Towers were used for military purposes, and in the case of a siege, people could find protection in them.

There was an urgency in David's cry because he was overwhelmed by what was happening, and he is fainting under the pressure. He was obviously not at the literal *"end of the earth,"* but he felt that way, for he was away from home and away from the sanctuary of God. For David, God's home was the tabernacle, the place where His glory dwelt, and David longed to be back in Jerusalem to worship and adore his Lord.

While you may not be running for your life as David did, you can still relate to this psalm. There are those times when you are overwhelmed by life and need God to intervene on your behalf. In such times, ask God to lead you to the Rock that is higher than you. In those times, the prelude of your prayer should remind you and God of all He is and all He has done. Declaring these things establishes precedent and fuels your prayer with the expectation that God will come through again.

> *"David knew God reigned from His exalted throne, high above every situation, and had the ability to deliver every time."*

Purposeful prayer (v.4-7)

The imagery of dwelling in the tent goes back to the desert experience when the Lord resided among the tribes of Israel in a tent, also referred to as the Tabernacle. It is this symbol of faith that the psalmist draws on as though to say, *"I will abide in thy tabernacle for ever."* David knows God is with him in trouble and will deliver him out of trouble!

And this is not the first, or only, psalm where David expresses this desire to dwell in God's house forever. (Psalm 23:6 and 27:4). For David, there was no better place to be, but in the presence of God.

After declaring his fear of the Lord and reaffirming his vows to Him, David confidently states his expectations of God. He expects that God will prolong his life, preserving him with His mercy and truth (v.6-7). David also expects that *"he shall abide before God for ever,"* revealing his desire to spend eternity with God.

Praise in prayer (v.8)

Thanksgiving is the response of the heart to the mighty acts of God. The praise of the Lord is to be a daily act, not just once or twice a week. When you add praise to your prayers, you cement and solidify them with something beautiful that moves the heart of God.

Maybe you've seen someone post or heard someone preach, "It's your season! It's your time!" The problem with such statements is that they only encourage you to receive promotion but fail to equip you to go through the process.

How do you handle it when it's not your season or not your time? Anyone can praise God after the storm is over, but those who can praise God during the storm are in a completely different category.

Praising God at the end of your prayer session is not hype; it's hope in God that He heard your cry and will bring you out in His perfect timing.

"Thanksgiving is the response of the heart to the mighty acts of God."

Conclusion

The psalm opens with David crying out in distress but closes with him singing praise to God. As David hid himself in The Rock, he placed his trust in God.

Jesus is the Rock of Ages, in whom born-again believers must hide themselves by faith. Christ alone is your refuge in the storms of life. If you feel like you've lost, or are losing something, remember that although trees lose their leaves every Fall, they still stand tall, waiting for Spring to come again (Isaiah 26:3-4).

You Are God Alone
Psalm 62

Chapter 22

Psalm 62 is focused on the theme of trusting God while in trouble. Through each verse, David teaches us how to navigate through the process and not just live for the promotion. Psalm 62 is not linked to a specific event, at least not that we are aware of. The inscription simply states, *"To the chief Musician, to Jeduthun, A Psalm of David."*

Psalm 62 teaches us that no person, pursuit, passion, or possession should ever take preeminence over God! God alone must be our trust! As he wrote this song, David declared that amid his troubles, he was not looking to anyone or anything other than

God to deliver him. Three times David uses the word *"only"* to indicate that he trusts in God alone to bring him through (v.2, 5-6).

David states that his faith rests solely in God, the singular object of his trust. This solitary reliance upon the Lord was the firm foundation for David's life. The message of Psalm 62 is clear: No matter how difficult the trial, trust in God alone.

"David declared that in the midst of his troubles, he was not looking to anyone or anything other than God to deliver him."

I will not be shaken (v.1-4)

In an interesting twist of irony, instead of presenting the problem first, David opened with praise and worship. Before he made one request, before he explained why he was trusting in God, he first declared he would not be shaken.

Although his enemies outnumbered him and tried to kill him, David did not waiver. David's enemies attempted to overthrow him, spreading their gossip and lies behind his back. They were two-faced, speaking kindly to him in person, but cursing him inwardly.

Yet, despite their actions and words, David remains firm, trusting in God alone. He refuses to vacillate in his faith. He knows God is his Rock and defense.

If your trust is in the government, and the government fails, you may fail with it. But, if your trust is in God, who never fails, you also will never fail.

You cannot allow anything or anyone to cause you to be shaken, to swerve from the faith, or to shipwreck your faith. Both the Old and New Testaments declare plainly that you must love the Lord your God with all your heart, soul, mind, and strength. If you will give your all to God, you will benefit from His all.

Plant your roots deep into His Word. Secure those roots with others of like precious faith. And when the storms of life come, you will be strong and will endure, for God and His Church will be with you in trouble.

"If your trust is in the government, and the government fails, you may fail with it. But, if your trust is in God, who never fails, you also will never fail."

I will wait in silence (v.5-8)

Some Bible translations interpret verse 5 to say, *"wait quietly,"* implying to wait in silence. The silence suggested here is David refusing to take matters into his own hands. He will not refute his enemies' claims. Instead, David will let God speak on his behalf. In this troubling time, and in his patient silence, David once again affirms His trust and hope in God alone.

Maybe the world we live in today could learn from such an ancient lesson. Far too many enjoy saints posting about their troubles instead of waiting quietly upon the Lord. Maybe you should keep your soul in silence toward the world, and instead pour your heart out to the Lord. I'm not suggesting you should be fake or even deny the reality of being gossiped or lied about. But please be careful with whom you pour your heart out to, and how much information you share. Hear and heed David's words, *"Trust in him at all times, ye people, pour out your heart before him: God is a refuge for us. Selah."*

You do need the support of others, so do not think I am suggesting you become a loner, handling things by yourself. Share your hurts with your pastor, a trustworthy born-again believer, and even a counselor if you need one; yet be careful what you share on social media.

I AM is Sovereign (v.9-12)

David trusted in God alone, because God alone is the only wise God! He alone is Sovereign. He alone is the Righteous Judge. If you put your trust in God alone, you will never fall. God is Sovereign over everything and everyone. Who better to trust than Him?

In these final four verses of Psalm 62, David contrasts the finite weakness of man against the illimitable strength of God. Frankly, there is no comparison, for *"men of high degree are a lie."* They appear to be powerful, yet they are worthless.

These supposed powerful enemies of David gained their wealth by extortion and put their hope and trust in their wealth. But David put his hope and trust in God alone.

Jeremiah gives us similar and wise advice, stating, *"Blessed is the man that trusteth in the LORD, and whose hope the LORD is. For he shall be as a tree planted by the waters..."* (17:7-8). Jeremiah goes on to explain that the roots of this tree shall reach deep into the fertile soil, producing an abundant harvest. This tree shall not be adversely affected by the summer heat or periods of drought; instead, the leaves will remain green, and *"never stop producing fruit"* (Jeremiah 17:8, New Living Translation).

Put your trust and hope in God alone. God never fails, never forsakes, and it is impossible for Him to lie. This world is passing away, but the one who trusts and hopes in God, obeying and doing His will, abides forever (1 John 2:17)!

> *"God never fails, never forsakes, and it is impossible for Him to lie."*

Conclusion

Like David in Psalm 62, Habakkuk also learned that trusting in God was truly his only option. When conflicted by the sin of Israel, and God's choice to use a heathen nation to punish Israel, Habakkuk complained. Yet, he also affirmed to God that he would continue serving, awaiting God's correction. God rewarded Habakkuk's waiting and affirmed His sovereignty. In the final lyrics of his song of prayer, Habakkuk wrote, *"The LORD God is my strength"* (Habakkuk 3:19).

I've learned the best option is to let God fight my battles. There have been times when I've tried to fight them by myself, and God allowed me to do that; however, I discovered that was never the best option. When I wait on God, trusting and hoping in Him alone, I always come out ahead.

Epilogue
by Paul Kinney

Moving with our 4-year-old daughter and 4-month-old son, we arrived in a small town in a different state; elected as the 27-year-old Pastor of a Pentecostal church. A man from the church was so kind and gracious, that he used his livestock trailer to move our furniture from Indianapolis to the apartment provided by the church.

Our first pastorate! We were excited! After having several pastors in my home church during my childhood, our intentions were to stay in this tiny town until Jesus came for his church!

I became acquainted with people, drove a school bus part time, began reaching the teens connected with the church and started a Home Bible Study. After serving as a youth leader, and then evangelizing for a year, we were home at last, ready to serve the Lord and do His work.

We preached! We visited! We loved people! We reached for backsliders, trying to connect with them! We worked on the church building, making improvements and repairs! The Church was our life. We made small changes in the church as we prayed and preached for revival. Teenagers began to pray in the altars. We baptized one teenager plus some adults. We were going to have revival!

Unfortunately, the changes and our youthful zeal upset some of the older people in the congregation. Some loved us because of our care and our zeal. Others began to hate us.

We took a trip to visit my parents. Upon our return to our church where we served as Pastor, a middle-aged couple who loved us, came to visit us. They were appointed to bring us the message that the church wanted us to leave. We were devastated. Brokenhearted! Physically sick!

My presbyter said, "Bro Kinney, we could fight this and win, but sometimes it's better to do what you need to do to save your family."

We could not afford to leave. We lived from each $100 paycheck from the church to the next week's $100 paycheck. I met with the church board, told them our financial predicament and they were glad to pay us our back pay to finance our leaving.

They paid us and my dad borrowed an old farm grain truck from my brother-in-law and drove 570 miles one way to load up our furniture and move us back home. We tucked our tail between our legs and ran for safety. As we drove away from the church apartment where we lived, we watched as they drove up to check out the apartment.

My wife and I were broken and decided that we would never pastor again. We had been hired and fired in 15 months! We returned to my hometown, I got a job and began to help in the church where my dad was the pastor.

Six months later, we received word that the church in Canton, Missouri needed a Pastor. The broken couple, who had decided to never pastor again, began to pray and consider Canton, Missouri. Two months later, in 1982, we moved to Canton and began having services in our single car garage.

The road has not always been easy, but we served as Pastor for over thirty-five years, and now as Bishop for the past three years. God restored what the cankerworm had eaten. He has blessed us and taken care of us. We are blessed far more than we deserve!

> *"God restored what the cankerworm had eaten."*

In Canton, Missouri, we were honored to serve as Pastor for Myron Powell during his last three years of high school. God gave us many others who have loved us and been faithful to the church and to us. When we didn't know if God could hear us or not, but He was always there, covering us with His Spirit and guiding our steps each day, and we're thankful.

In Myron Powell's third volume of the Book of Psalms, you will discover how to trust God, even if you've been through a difficult situation such as I have just shared. If you trust God during the process, He will bring you safely through, just like He brought my wife and I safely through, restoring and blessing us abundantly and exceedingly.

Paul F. Kinney
Bishop, Life Tabernacle
Canton, MO

Other volumes in this series:

In volume one, two main choices are revealed. You can choose right or wrong, heaven or hell. Choose wisely; you only live forever.
Available on Amazon.

In volume two, the trustworthiness of God is revealed. God never fails, never forsakes, and cannot lie. God can be trusted every time.
Available on Amazon.

More volumes coming soon:
    Vol. 4–*Impartial Praise*–Psalms 63-79
    Vol. 5–*The LORD of the Lockdown*–Psalms 80-98
    Vol. 6–*God Our Salvation*–Psalms 99-118
    Vol. 7–*A Life Well Lived*–Psalm 119
    Vol. 8–*The Songs of Degrees*–Psalms 120-134
    Vol. 9–*The Heart of Worship*–Psalms 135-150

Made in the USA
Monee, IL
08 September 2021